Obama Won,
but Romney *Almost* Was President

How the Democrats Targeted Electoral College
Votes to Win the 2012 Presidential Election

❧ ❧ ❧ ❧ ❧

A Historical Analysis of Every U.S. Presidential Election
and the Events That Influenced Them

Everett E. Murdock PhD

H.O.T. Press

H.O.T. Press
Los Angeles, California
www.hotpresspublishing.com
Established 1984

ISBN: 0-923178-14-7
ISBN-13: 978-0-923178-14-7

For Zoe,
Without whom this book would not exist,
and without whom I would not exist.

Acknowledgments

I had planned to acknowledge all of the books on U.S. history that provided me with background information while I was writing this book, but I soon realized that would be an impossible task because I've been reading books on U.S. history all my life. Let me just say I am truly indebted to anybody who has written anything about U.S. history. I assume they did it simply because they are, like me, interested in the history of our country.

I am also indebted to those who took the time to put information about U.S. history on the internet. Once again, I started to list them, but found the list growing into the hundreds (and even then I knew I was leaving a bunch of them out). So I will just say this: if you've ever put anything about U.S. history on the internet, I probably read it while researching this book, and I am therefore, indebted to you.

Contents

Introduction
He Who Wins May Lose

It's a tried-and-true old saying: if you want to know what the future will bring, study the past. Studying the past, we learn that **in four U.S. presidential elections, the candidate who won the most votes did not get to be president**.

In the spring of 2012, President Obama's popularity was waning, and the Republican Party had quite overtly stated that their number one goal was to make Obama a one-term president. It looked like the 2012 presidential election was going to be a close race.

At that time, I began writing a book about how we elect our presidents, with a focus on the Electoral College. I decided to give it the speculative title of *Obama Will Win, but Romney Will Be President.* That book was published in May, and it suggested that if the states that traditionally voted Republican went back to doing so in 2012, the candidate that won the most votes in the general election might not get to be president.

As it turned out, President Obama won both the popular vote and the Electoral College, but the voting in key swing states was the closest in U.S. history.

In the last close presidential election, **Al Gore won the general election vote by 543,895 votes**, but George Bush got to be president. Why? Because despite Gore's win of the popular vote, Bush got five more votes than Gore in the Electoral College, accumulating 271 electoral votes, only one vote more than the 270 required to be elected president.

In this follow-up book, written in the days after the 2012 presidential election, I will describe how our present system of electing our presidents evolved, and I will analyze each of the nation's past presidential elections. In each case, I will discuss the role the

Electoral College system played in determining who got to be president.

With that background in mind, I will discuss, in detail, what happened in the presidential election of 2012 and how it *almost* turned out to be a repeat of what happened in 2000 when the candidate that won the general election didn't get to be president.

Chapter One
The Origins of the Electoral College System

How is it possible that a candidate can win the popular vote and yet not be elected president? The answer lies within the archaic and complex structure of something known as **the Electoral College** which is a system of selecting **electors** who cast the votes that actually count.

Most Americans can't understand why we need an Electoral College. They ask why they can't just vote for president like they vote for every other political office. Public opinion polls repeatedly show most Americans favor abolishing the Electoral College.

There have been more than 700 proposals introduced in Congress to reform or eliminate the Electoral College. **In fact, more constitutional amendments have been introduced regarding the Electoral College than on any other subject. But they all failed**. After 236 years, Americans still do not get to vote for their president.

The fact is, not only is the Electoral College system nonsensical, it is **biased and unfair**. There have been several times in this country's history when the members of the Electoral College have not voted for the candidate that won the popular vote. Most Americans find this incomprehensible. They don't understand how the winner of the general election can be denied the presidency.

Another thing many Americans *do not know* is that according to the U.S. Constitution, the electors *do not* have to vote for the candidate that won their state in the general election. It's true. When the Electoral College meets, the electors can vote for whoever they want to. They can vote for the candidate that lost their state in the general election, or anybody else. The person they vote for does not even have to be a presidential candidate. **In the past, many electors have decided *not to* vote for the candidate the voters of their state chose**. The U.S. Constitution, places no restrictions on who members of the Electoral College cast their votes for.

At least Americans can take solace in the fact that the winner of the national election *usually* turns out to be the same candidate that wins the general election. In the 57 presidential elections that have been held in the United States so far, the Electoral College chose a different president than the one the people chose **only nine percent of the time**. But is that a good track record for something so important? Should the citizens of the United States be satisfied that the candidate who wins the general election *usually* gets to be president?

As we shall see, the dramatic difference in the outcome of the popular vote and the outcome of the Electoral College vote in both the 2000 and 2012 elections are only the latest examples of how the Electoral College system can go wrong, and there are strong indications it is going to happen more often in the future.

How We Got into This Mess

To understand how the strange and problematic Electoral College system of choosing presidents came about, we first have to consider the fragile political structure of our young nation as it was trying to free itself from Britain.

By 1733, thirteen British colonies had been established along the eastern seaboard of North America. They were: Connecticut, Delaware, Georgia, Maryland, Massachusetts Bay, New Hampshire, New Jersey, New York, North Carolina, Pennsylvania, Rhode Island and Providence Plantations, South Carolina, and Virginia.

To a great degree, the thirteen colonies had always been more or less self governing; therefore, there was widespread resentment whenever the British tried to impose taxes or enforce special rules that created hardships for the colonists. Over time, there were increasing protests against British rule. The most famous of the protests was the **Boston Tea Party** where a group of colonists made their resentment of a recently imposed British tea tax known by dumping a large amount of British-owned tea into the Boston harbor.

In 1774, representatives of twelve of the thirteen colonies (all except Georgia) met in Philadelphia to discuss what to do about the British crackdowns that were happening in response to the protests.

In that first meeting, which became known as the **first continental congress**, the colonists could not come to an agreement about what to do about the situation. Members such as George Washington and Patrick Henry from Virginia, John Adams and Samuel Adams from Massachusetts, and John Dickinson from Pennsylvania, were not willing to take the position that the colonies should break away from British rule. They just wanted more self rule. The delegates to the congress put together a petition asking the British Parliament to address the colonists' grievances.

When the British were unwilling to agree to *any* of the colonist requests, a second congress was called to decide what to do next. This time, the meeting took on a greater sense of urgency because some militia groups in Massachusetts had already engaged British soldiers in armed conflict. Moderates among the delegates wanted to continue to try to find an accord with the British, but many of the delegates believed it was time to prepare for war. In the end, they did both. They sent another petition to Britain with a request for less taxation and more self rule, but just in case, they also began putting together an army.

The King of England refused to even read the petition. He declared the colonists rebels and sent troops to quell "the rebellion." Thus began **the Revolutionary War**.

The Articles of Confederation and the United States Constitution

After much debate, the delegates representing the thirteen colonies put together **articles of confederation** which declared the United States of America to be a confederation of sovereign states. The Articles of Confederation served as the new nation's constitution until a **constitutional convention** was convened in 1787 to lay out a governing structure. The document that came out of that convention was the **United States Constitution**.

Getting agreement as to how the new government should be organized was not an easy task. There was considerable controversy about the issue of slavery and much disagreement about how members of the governing bodies should be elected. Even after they had agreed to maintain the British concept of a two-house legislature, there was great difficulty in deciding how the two houses should be structured. Eventually, it was decided that the **House of Representatives** would be apportioned according to the population of a state (the total population, not just voters or legal citizens). But there was much contention about how the states with smaller populations would be represented in the government. Remember, the constitutional convention was made up of delegates from **each of the states**, meaning the least populated states had as much decision-making power at the convention as the more populous states. The delegates from the smaller states felt the larger states would dominate the government; therefore, they often refused to go along with the wishes of the larger states.

Finally, a compromise was worked out to give the smaller states more voting power: **the senate** would be made up of two senators *appointed* from each state, no matter how large or small the population of the state was.

Of course, the larger population states, especially the northern states, didn't like that idea one bit, because it meant states with much smaller populations would have equal clout in the Senate. But no other solution could be agreed upon, so that method was adopted.

Probably the most significant area of contention that arose regarding the apportioning of seats in the House of Representatives had to do with slaves. The southern slave-holding states wanted to count their millions of slaves as part of their apportionment even though the slaves were not considered to be citizens of the United States. But the larger northern states pointed out fact that the slaves were not legally citizens of the United States. There was also the issue of taxes. Because slaves were legally the property of the slave owner, the northern states said they should be taxed as property. The southern states disagreed, saying they were not property, but living beings. In other words, the southern states wanted to have it both ways.

Neither side was willing to budge and it looked as if the convention would be bogged down in the issue forever.

In what would be the first of many compromises with the southern slave states in order to get the government-making process moving again, it was decided, for purposes of representation in the House of

Representatives, slaves would count as three-fifth of a person. Known as **the Three-Fifths Compromise**, it was written into the United States Constitution as follows:

> Representatives and direct Taxes shall be apportioned among the several States which may be included within this Union, according to their respective Numbers, which shall be determined by adding to the whole Number of free Persons, including those bound to Service for a Term of Years, and excluding Indians not taxed, three-fifths of all other Persons.

It was a decision that would have long lasting effects. It is estimated that before the Civil War, there were about nine million free whites living in the South, as compared to about four million slaves. Based on the Three-Fifths Compromise, that meant the South was given credit for an extra 2,400,000 people when the number of seats in the House of Representatives were assigned.

It meant that the southern states not only were given disproportionate power in the Senate (two senators per state, the same number that was assigned to the much larger northern states), but also disproportionate power in the House of Representatives. It meant that if the apportionment was based on free population, the slave states should have been apportioned 33 seats in the House of Representatives. By including their slaves and counting them as three-fifth of a person, they got 47. It also meant, they were given more electors in the Electoral College (the number of electors is based on the number of legislators as state has). As a result, for many years, Southerners dominated the Presidency, the House of Representatives, and the Supreme Court.

COMMENT:

As a direct result of giving the South disproportionate voting power, ten of the first twelve presidents were slave holders. The first twelve president's status with regard to slave holding is listed below:

George Washington, the first president, was a wealthy Virginia plantation owner who owned more than 200 slaves before, during, and after he was president.

The second president, John Adams, was from Massachusetts which was not a slave state. However, some years before he became president, he was given a slave as a gift. He used her as the family cook.

Thomas Jefferson, the third president, owned a 5,000 acre plantation in Virginia and owned more than 100 slaves, including one woman, Sally Hemings, who was rumored to have been his mistress after his wife died. It was said she bore several of his children while he was president, all of whom, by law, remained slaves. Modern DNA evidence and analysis of the timing of his visits to his estate at Monticello seem to have proved the truth of that rumor.

James Madison, the fourth president, owned a large tobacco plantation in Virginia. He inherited hundreds of slaves and continued to hold them for the rest of his life.

James Monroe, the fifth president, was also a Virginia plantation owner and owned many slaves.

John Quincy Adams, the sixth president, being from Massachusetts was bared by state law from owning slaves.

Andrew Jackson, the seventh president, bought his first slave, a young woman, when he was only 21 years old. He later became a businessman and for a while was in the business of buying and selling slaves. At one time, he owned more than 300 slaves.

Martin Van Buren, the eighth president, was from a slave-holding family, but he personally owned only one slave.

William Henry Harrison, the ninth president, was from a Virginia plantation family that owned many slaves. Harrison was said to have illegally taken several of them with him when he traveled to states where slavery was against the law.

John Tyler, the tenth president, was also a Virginia tobacco plantation owner who owned many slaves.

James K. Polk, the eleventh president, was a slave holder from North Carolina.

Zachary Taylor, the twelfth president, was born into a slave-holding family in Virginia. Although he chose a military career, he held onto his slaves. While president, he held about 100 slaves.

After 1850, the rapidly increasing populations of the Northern states began to break the stranglehold the Southern states had on electing presidents. At the same time, owning slaves became much more controversial in the North. As a result, political candidates from the slave states tended to transfer their slaves to a relative before running for national office.

Originally, the only national office that was elected by public vote was the choosing of the states' members of the House of Representatives (and even then, only **males** were allowed to vote, and in many states, only **men who owned property could vote**).

Even the members of the U.S. Senate were selected by political leaders. The original method of **appointing senators rather than electing them** continued to be in force until 1913 when a constitutional amendment was proposed to require direct election of senators. Many political leaders fought against the proposed amendment, and it took a year before it was finally ratified by 37 states (one more state, Delaware, ratified it in 2010). Alabama, Florida, Georgia, Kentucky, Maryland, Mississippi, Rhode Island, South Carolina, and Virginia *did not* ratify it, and Utah made a point of *explicitly rejecting* it.

However, once it was made the law of the land, even the states that didn't ratify the new constitutional amendment had to allow direct election of senators.

COMMENT:

The difficulty of getting three-fourths of the states to ratify such a common-sense concept as direct election of senators *by the citizens of their state* probably tells us how difficult it would be to get three-fourths of the states to go along with the idea of getting rid of the Electoral College system of electing presidents and vice presidents.

Dispute over How the President Should Be Chosen

Perhaps the most contentious dispute at the original **constitutional convention** in 1787 revolved around how the president was to be elected. As a result, it was one of the last issues to be resolved.

Many of the delegates felt Congress should choose the president - or maybe even appoint a presiding **committee instead of a single president** - but the majority of the delegates felt the people ought to be allowed to elect their president.

The delegates from the smaller states and the slave states were dead set against allowing the people to elect the president. After much ongoing contentious debate, the founding fathers gave up on their idea of a popular vote for president. The delegates had two reasons for deciding against a popular vote:

1) The delegates from the smaller states and the southern slave states fought long and hard against the idea because they knew the more populous northern states would end up controlling the presidential elections.

2) Many of the delegates didn't trust the people to make the right decision.

The first point, that the smaller states would get outvoted by the states with larger populations, was true then and is still true today. Some states have much larger populations than others, and if the president was elected by popular vote, the larger-population states would have more say in who gets to be president. At the constitutional convention, the delegates from the smaller states felt their primary duty was to look out for the interests of their state. Each state, no matter how large or small, got a vote at the constitutional convention, and the delegates from the small southern states often voted together to stymie the wishes of the larger northern states. In the end, the larger-population northern states had to compromise with the smaller states and the slave states. That meant a system would have to be set up in which the smaller states would be given *more* voting power (proportionally) than the larger states. The delegates had already agreed to give the slave states more voting power in Congress, and in the end, this new compromise meant they also had to give them more power in electing the president and vice president.

The second point is understandable, but less defensible. There were a lot of reasons put forward as to why the president should not be directly elected by the people, but they all came down to the same point: **many delegates at the constitutional convention did not believe the people were informed enough to make such an important decision**. While the delegates believed the people had enough information to elect their state representatives, they did not believe the people understood federal and international issues well enough to choose their own Senators or their national leader.

The Compromise: Electors

After much haggling, the delegates came up with a compromise: the people *would not* be allowed to vote for their president; instead, the political leaders in each of the states would decide who would be president and vice president. The states would choose **electors** who would then get together with the electors from the other states to hash out who the president and vice president would be.

After even more haggling, the smaller states were given extra voting power by assigning **one electoral vote for each representative in the House, plus two more corresponding to each state's two senators**.

Of course, the delegates from the more populous states were not happy with the idea that the smaller states would get two extra electors that had nothing to do with how many voters there were in the state. In addition, it meant the southern states would get extra electors by including a count of their slaves in the assignment of representatives. It violated one of the most basic principles that guided the framers of the constitution, that all voters should be equal. (Today, legal scholars say the Electoral College could be ruled unconstitutional if it wasn't specifically laid out in the constitution.) Once again, the larger northern states were outvoted by the delegates from the smaller states and the slave states.

COMMENT:

Today, most U.S. citizens probably assume the members of the Electoral College are "guided" by the outcome of their state's general election. The truth is, there is no language in the U.S. Constitution to suggest that. There is nothing in the Constitution to even suggest that there should be public elections for president or vice president, and at first, most states did not hold presidential elections: in the first presidential election in 1789, only 6 of the 13 original states held any sort of popular vote for president. Whether or not an election for president was held, it was still the political leaders of the state simply that decided who they wanted to be president and then sent electors to the Electoral College meeting to express those wishes. They then were to send representatives to the electors meeting to express those wishes.

Understandably, the people of the United States were not happy that they had no say in who their president would be. They brought political heat to bear on the politicians to allow a popular vote. Eventually all the states began to hold general elections in which the people could cast votes for their preferences for president and vice president, **even though, under the Constitution, the popular election results had no legal status (and they still don't today)**.

Eventually, **some** states passed laws that stated an elector could be fined if he or she did not vote for the candidate that won their state's popular vote. Nevertheless, in the 57 past presidential elections, there have been **158 instances in which an elector *did not* vote for the popular vote winner**. These electors are referred to as "**faithless electors**." Later, I will discuss what motivated those 158 faithless electors.

To make sure the electors didn't just vote for their state's local candidate, it was written into the Constitution that the electors had to vote for at least one candidate from outside their state.

The votes of all the electors from the states would be tallied and added together, and the candidate that got the most votes would be named president. The candidate that came in second would be named vice president.

COMMENT:

The Constitution did not state that the electors had to vote for the candidate the people preferred. The electors were supposed to vote for whoever the leaders in the states wanted. As stated in the Constitution, a candidate has to gain an absolute majority of the state electors or else the decision gets sent to the House of Representatives. Some have speculated that the framers of the Constitution assumed that such an approach would result in a variety of candidates being put forward by the electors, meaning no one candidate would have the required majority and the decision would come back to the House, the body of Congress in which the number of members are determined by state populations. That way, the wishes of the people would be better served (through the representatives they elected). In other words, the vote of the state electors would be considered **nominations** from which the House of Representatives would choose a president and vice president.

But it didn't turn out that way. The Electoral College (the term "Electoral College" does not appear in the Constitution but began to appear in newspapers sometime in the early 1800s) was created at a time when political parties did not exist. The framers of the Constitution did not anticipate the emergence of political parties. When two political parties emerged in the late 1700s, the **Federalists** and the **Democratic-Republicans**, they immediately got involved in the selection of electors. It was crucial for both political parties to *try* to make sure the electors they chose were loyal **to their party** and that they would vote the way the party wanted them to.

Today, the two main political parties in the United States, the **Democrats** and the **Republicans**, pretty much control the election process. As a result, presidential elections now almost always come down to a face-off between the candidates nominated by those two parties. So far, the two major parties have been able to squeeze out any other candidates. For that reason, one of the major party candidates usually wins the required absolute majority of the Electoral College votes, and therefore the decision never gets sent to the House of Representatives. If a third party candidate was to get a significant number of electoral votes, no candidate would get an absolute majority of electoral votes and the decision would be sent to the House of Representatives.

The rules of the Electoral College system can't be changed without changing the U.S. Constitution. That would require a constitutional amendment to pass both houses of congress and the approval of three-fourths of the states. Of course, that would mean the states with fewer voters would have to give up their proportional voting advantage. Most observers think that is unlikely to happen.

A rule was written into the Constitution to keep electors from voting for their own local friends. It says electors cannot vote for a president and vice president from the same state. Although that requirement is still in the Constitution, it has been all but forgotten In the election of 2000, the Republican nominee for president, George Bush, and the Republican nominee for vice president, Dick Cheney, were both from Texas.

Today the electors in 48 of the 50 states (all except Maine and Nebraska) are *supposed to* (but not required to) give 100% of the electoral votes to the candidate who wins a state's popular vote. A candidate who wins the popular vote, even if it's only **by a single vote, gets *all* of that state's electoral votes**. That means, when the Electoral College members vote, **the votes the less popular candidate received in the general election are thrown out**. It is as if those people never voted at all.

This "winner-take-all" method is not written into the Constitution, but with the emergence of political parties, more states began to adopt the winner-take-all method in order to give their state more control over the election process. That decision was to shape all presidential elections to come.

After all the compromises had been hashed out, each state was allotted one Electoral College member equal to the number of seats the state had in the House of Representatives. In addition, each state got two more Electoral College members to represent the state's two senators.

Below is the wording of that section as it was written into the Constitution:

> Each State shall appoint, in such Manner as the Legislature thereof may direct, a Number of Electors, equal to the whole Number of Senators and Representatives to which the State may be entitled in the Congress: but no Senator or Representative, or Person holding an Office of Trust or Profit under the United States, shall be appointed an Elector.

The method of selecting electors was left vague. It simply said "the states" would choose their electors and those electors would get together to choose the president and vice president. Below is the wording of that section as it was written into the Constitution:

> The Electors shall meet in their respective States, and vote by Ballot for two Persons, of whom one at least shall not be an Inhabitant of the same State with themselves. And they shall make a List of all the Persons voted for, and of the Number of Votes for each; which List they shall sign and certify, and transmit sealed to the Seat of the Government of the United States, directed to the President of the Senate. The President of the Senate shall, in the Presence of the Senate and House of Representatives, open all the Certificates, and the Votes shall then be counted. The Person having the greatest Number of Votes shall be the President, if such Number be a Majority of the whole Number of Electors appointed; and if there be more than one who have such Majority, and have an equal Number of Votes, then the House of Representatives shall immediately chuse by Ballot one of them for President; and if no Person have a Majority, then from the five highest on the List the said House shall in like

Manner chuse the President. But in chusing the President, the Votes shall be taken by States, the Representation from each State having one Vote; A quorum for this Purpose shall consist of a Member or Members from two thirds of the States, and a Majority of all the States shall be necessary to a Choice. In every Case, after the Choice of the President, the Person having the greatest Number of Votes of the Electors shall be the Vice President. But if there should remain two or more who have equal Votes, the Senate shall chuse from them by Ballot the Vice President.

As you can see, there is no provision for assessing the people's wishes. It was just left up to "the states."

COMMENT:

As more states were added to the Union, the number of members in the Electoral College increased, and in 1961, a constitutional amendment (the Twenty-Third Amendment) allotted three Electoral College votes to the District of Columbia.

Today, the total number of members of the Electoral College has been permanently set at 538. How many electors each state gets is rebalanced after every census. (Note that the rebalancing is based on the *census*, not on the number of voters or even on the number of legal residents in the state. As a result, states that have had an influx of illegal immigrants have been gaining electoral votes, and the states whose populations have not been growing in population have been losing electoral votes.) Half of 538 is 269. That means, to win the presidency, a candidate must win 270 Electoral College votes (the majority).

How Well Has the Electoral College System Worked?

In the nation's 57 past presidential elections, the Electoral College method of selecting the president has concurred with the popular vote 93% of the time.

You might ask, only 93%? Shouldn't the winner of the popular vote *always* get to be president?

Yes, but then there would be no need for the Electoral College. The truth is, as we shall see, the Electoral College system is so archaic and so flawed, it's kind of surprising it only fails seven percent of the time.

The sections that follow describe each of the U.S. presidential elections, what influenced them, and the role the Electoral College played in the outcome.

Chapter Two
Presidential Elections without Popular Elections

The Presidential Election of 1788

In the first presidential election, in 1788, **George Washington, a Virginia planter and slave holder, was expected to win**. He had led the country's military through the hard times of the **Revolutionary War** as commander-in-chief of the **Continental Army**, and most of the leaders in the states felt he deserved to be the first president.

When the electors ballots were counted, Washington had received 69 electoral votes and John Adams got 34. Based on the Constitution's electoral rules, that meant Washington would be president, and Adams, the person who came in second, would be vice president.

The Presidential Election of 1792

In the second presidential election, held in 1792, Washington was again expected to win, and again John Adams got the second most number of electoral votes (which now included electors from the two new states, Kentucky and Vermont), so they continued in office.

The Presidential Election of 1796

In the third presidential election, held in 1796, Washington chose not to run for reelection. Therefore, there *was* contention for the office and the emergence of political parties played a big role in the election.

Vice President John Adams ran for the office as a representative of the newly formed **Federalist** Party. Former Secretary of State Thomas Jefferson and Senator Aaron Burr ran on the **Democratic-Republican** ticket.

The original political party, the Federalists believed the United States should maintain good relations with Britain. They had negotiated, in 1794, a treaty with Britain known as **the Jay Treaty**.

The Democratic-Republican Party, on the other hand, was **a states' rights party** bent on limiting federal power. They were strongly opposed the Jay Treaty as well as most of the other Federalist policies.

The Federalist Party - originally the *only* American political party - believed the United States should maintain good relations with Britain and negotiated, in 1794, a treaty with Britain that became known as **the Jay Treaty**.

The Democratic-Republican Party, on the other hand, was **a states' rights party** bent on limiting federal power. They were strongly opposed the Jay Treaty as well as most of the other Federalist policies.

The Federalists found most of their support in New England and in the larger cities, while the Democratic-Republicans found support in the rural south.

In seven of the states, Connecticut, Delaware, New Jersey, New York, Rhode Island, South Carolina, and Vermont, the electors were chosen by the state legislatures. That meant whichever party controlled a state's legislature controlled the selection of electors.

In some states, general elections were held to vote for electors that had to state publicly which candidate they favored.

In four states, Kentucky, Maryland, North Carolina, and Virginia, the voters in each congressional district in the state got to vote for one elector.

Georgia and Pennsylvania held a statewide election to select electors.

Massachusetts, New Hampshire, and Tennessee used a combination of general election approaches.

The political leaders of the states were not bound by the outcome of those popular votes, but it is generally believed they helped the electors understand which candidate the people favored.

The vote of the Electoral College in 1796 was close, with 71 votes going to Adams and 68 going to Jefferson. By rule, that meant John Adams would be president, and his opponent, Thomas Jefferson, would be vice president. It would be the only time in U.S. history that the president and the vice president came from different parties.

Chapter Three
Political Parties Evolve

The Presidential Election of 1800

Details of the 1800 presidential election read like a fictional novel of intrigue, and much of the intrigue was due to the structure of the Electoral College.

The advent of popular voting was seen as influencing the state electors. As a result, a few of the candidates actually campaigned. They got on their horses (literally as well as figuratively) and set out to meet the voters.

Today, we are so used to national presidential campaigning it is hard to imagine that not much national campaigning took place in the early presidential elections. Politics was something that was done in Philadelphia (the Capital at that time).

The emergence of two opposing political parties in the 1796 election set the stage for a new level of antagonism in the 1800 election. The Federalist party put up John Adams for president and Charles Pickney for vice president, while the Democratic-Republican party put up Thomas Jefferson for president and Aaron Burr for vice president.

Most of the antagonism was over the Federalist's continuing alignment with Britain and their plan to build up a centralized federal government, including the raising of an army, possibly to help Britain in its ongoing war with France.

Despite the Federalist's well-entrenched position in the seat of national power (President Washington did not belong to either party, but supported the Federalists), the Democratic-Republicans were better organized at the local level.

A long and bitter campaign for electoral votes ensued and established many of the campaigning methods we see in modern presidential elections, including the invention of **the smear campaign.** Jefferson was philosophical about man's role in the world so the Federalists tried to paint him as against religion. They claimed God was on their side and said a vote for Adams was a vote for God and a religious presidency, while a vote for Jefferson would be a vote against God.

In this election of 1800, the Democratic-Republicans tried to paint the Federalists as against the common man and in favor of the rich and powerful (sound familiar?). They also attacked the **Alien and Sedition Acts** that had been passed by the Federalists in congress and signed by the Federalist President Adams. The acts, supposedly enacted because of a perceived threat from France made it more difficult for immigrants to become a U.S. citizen, and gave the president the power to deport immigrants if they were deemed "dangerous to the peace and safety of the United States." The acts also gave the president the power to limit freedom of speech, again if in the president's opinion such speech was "dangerous to the peace and safety of the United States." The Democratic-Republican attack on the acts was fairly successful because many citizens felt the acts went too far, especially when most people felt the chance of an attack from France was unlikely. The Democratic-Republicans said some aspects of the acts were clearly unconstitutional in that they violated the first amendment which states, "Congress shall make no law respecting an establishment of religion, or prohibiting the free exercise thereof; or abridging the freedom of speech, or of the press; or the right of the people peaceably to assemble, and to petition the Government for a redress of grievances." However, all of the members of the Supreme Court were Federalists, all appointed by Washington, so most people felt there was no chance of getting the court to overturn the acts even if they were blatantly unconstitutional.

Jefferson came right out and said the acts were created as a way to keep the Federalists in power by quashing any criticism, and in fact, the Federalists did use the acts and the threat of war to restrict what newspapers printed. They had some newspaper editors arrested and their newspapers shut down. The newspapers that were shut down were almost always publications that leaned toward the Democratic-Republicans, and this was especially important because at that time, newspapers were just beginning to play a more important role than word of mouth.

One result of the Democratic-Republican fight against the Alien and Sedition Acts was that they had considerable success in getting the newly arrived immigrants on their side, especially those from France and Ireland. It was the first election in which candidates tried to appeal to **special interest groups**.

There was also a great deal of focus on the Electoral College. Both sides saw the flaws in the Electoral College system and so they tried to manipulate those flaws to their own advantage. Both political parties also promised significant political favors to states that could swing electoral votes their way.

One or the more notable manipulation of electoral votes occurred during this 1800 election. Virginia was one of the states in which the voters **in each congressional district** voted for one elector. Thomas Jefferson realized that if his home state of Virginia would have allocated **all** of its electoral votes to him in the 1796 election, he would have been elected president. Therefore, before the 1800 election, he convinced the Virginia state legislature to change to a system in which the candidate that won the most electors, got **all** the electors. It became known as the **winner-take-all** system of allocating electoral votes.

Later, other states would realize they would have to do the same or else states that used the winner-take-all method would have more power in presidential elections. Over the next fifty years, it became the standard way of allocating electoral votes in almost all of the states (today, only Maine and Nebraska still allocate electoral votes proportionally).

In 1800, each state could choose its own election day. Therefore, the election that year went on for seven months. The last state to vote was South Carolina, and the word went out that Adams and Jefferson were tied in the Electoral College. The electors from South Carolina were solidly behind the Democratic-Republican party meaning Jefferson and Burr were going to win the national election. Therefore, a plan was hatched to have the South Carolina electors withhold one vote from Burr to make sure Jefferson would be president and Burr would come in second, making him the vice president (remember, electors had to vote for two candidates). No one knows what went wrong, but all of the South Carolina electors ended up voting for *both* Jefferson and Burr meaning the tie vote was maintained, and that meant neither candidate had a majority. As stipulated in the Electoral College section of the Constitution, the decision about who would be president was sent to the House of Representatives.

One simple solution would have been for Burr to withdraw from consideration, but he refused.

When the election of the president goes to the House of Representatives, a candidate has to get an absolute majority of the **states** (not a majority of the representatives) to be elected president. Nine of the sixteen states would have to come to an agreement.

The **lame duck** Federalists in the House of Representatives did not have enough power to swing the election their way, but they did have enough votes to keep the Democratic-Republicans from electing their candidates.

Ballot after ballot was taken with no clear winner. Days went by with no movement by either side.

At some point, the Federalists began to vote for Burr, apparently taking on an **anybody-but-Jefferson** attitude. It was clear, if this went on, nobody was going to win. It was quite possible that *there would be no president.* That presented a dire situation because the Constitution had no contingency for such an outcome (and still doesn't today).

After 34 ballots with neither side budging, everybody in Congress knew the electoral collage process was a complete failure. But because the process was mandated by the U.S. Constitution, Congress couldn't do anything about it. To change the Electoral College system, they would have to pass a bill amend the Constitution and get three-fourths of the state to ratify it. They knew the South would not give up the advantage they had in the Electoral College, so that was not a viable option.

Meanwhile, word about the stalemate in the House of Representatives was leaking out. People were upset about the whole flawed Electoral College system of electing their president. First, the people had not had any say in the election, and now their representatives in Congress seemed to be engaged in partisan squabbling that was going nowhere.

In Congress, there were rumors of armed bands of citizens marching on the capital to take things into their own hands. It was said they were coming to demand, by force of arms if need be, that Jefferson, the candidate they had voted for, be named president.

Finally, in response to what was clearly turning out to be dangerous situation, Jefferson approached the Federalist leaders and gave them assurances that he would not completely wipe out everything they had accomplished during the twelve years they had been in power. In response, in preparation for the 35th ballot, Federalist Party leader Alexander Hamilton (who strongly disliked Burr) allowed a few moderate Federalists to change their votes from Burr to Jefferson and Jefferson was elected president. Burr, having come in second, had to settle for the vice presidency.

COMMENT:

Some have speculated that the framers of the Constitution anticipated that the election of the president would often be decided by the House of Representatives, and that was what they wanted. But it seems more likely that they just hadn't considered the possibility that political parties would emerge. They couldn't have realized that political parties would complicate the presidential election process as they fought with each other for advantage.

However, the framers of the Constitution did provide a mechanism for changing it. They built in an amendment process. But they didn't want the Constitution they had so carefully crafted to be easy to change, so they stipulated that it would take agreement in Congress *and* agreement among three-fourths of the states to change it. They couldn't have realized how hard it would be to get that many states to agree on anything.

Chapter Four
Flaws in the Electoral College System

The disastrous election of 1800 started a debate in Congress about how to "fix" the Electoral College system. The debate was wide ranging and often contentious, but it was only focused on finding a solution to what had happened in the most recent election, the tie in the Electoral College that had sent the election to the House of Representatives. There was no mention of needing a popular vote, no discussion of changing how the electors were to be chosen, and no mention of electors being required by law to vote for the candidate that had won the popular vote.

Despite the obvious flaws in the Electoral College system, it was clear that the politicians of that era did not want the decision about who would be president to be in the hands of the people.

The result of the congressional deliberations was a proposal to amend the Electoral College section of the Constitution. The proposed an amendment that simply stipulated that electors should make separate choices for president and vice president.

The **Twelfth Amendment** to the Constitution was proposed by the Congress on December 9, 1803 and was ratified on June 15, 1804, just in time for the 1804 presidential election.

Below is the full text of the Twelfth Amendment:

The Electors shall meet in their respective states, and vote by ballot for President and Vice-President, one of whom, at least, shall not be an inhabitant of the same state with themselves; they shall name in their ballots the person voted for as President, and in distinct ballots the person voted for as Vice-President, and they shall make distinct lists of all persons voted for as President, and of all persons voted for as Vice-President, and of the number of votes for each, which lists they shall sign and certify, and transmit sealed to the seat of the government of the United States, directed to the President of the Senate; The President of the Senate shall, in the presence of the Senate and House of Representatives, open all the certificates and the votes shall then be counted;- The person having the greatest number of votes for President, shall be the President, if such number be a majority of the whole number of Electors appointed; and if no person have such majority, then from the persons having the highest numbers not exceeding three on the list of those voted for as President, the House of Representatives shall choose immediately, by ballot, the President. But in choosing the President, the votes shall be taken by states, the representation from each state having one vote; a quorum for this purpose shall consist of a member or members from two-thirds of the states, and a majority of all the states shall be necessary to a choice.... The person having the greatest number of votes as Vice-President, shall be the Vice-President, if such number be a majority of the whole number of Electors appointed, and if no person have a majority, then from the two highest numbers on the list, the Senate shall choose the Vice-President; a quorum for the purpose shall consist of two-thirds of the whole number of senators, and a majority of the whole number shall be necessary to a choice. But no person constitutionally ineligible to the office of President shall be eligible to that of Vice-President to the United States.

Notice that the Twelfth Amendment made few changes to the original language regarding how the president and vice president are chosen. It still *does not* say, or *even suggest*, that electors should vote for the winner of the popular vote. In fact, **it still doesn't even suggest there needs to be a popular vote.**

COMMENT:

When the first few presidents were chosen, only a few states held general elections. The decision about who would be president was pretty much up to the political leaders in the states. Then they selected electors who would vote that way.

Although Americans now take the election of a president very seriously, voting for the president in an public election is not even mentioned in the Constitution. However, some states (not all) have passed laws that say the members of the state's slate of electors **have to** vote for the winner of that state's general presidential election. However, the most the state can do is levy a fine on an elector who disobeys that *suggestion.* (Some legal scholars say such laws are unconstitutional because there is nothing in the Electoral College section of the U.S. Constitution that says an elector has to vote in any specified way.) There is much ado about today's presidential elections, and untold amounts of money are spent on trying to get Americans to vote for one candidate or another, the results of that voting have no legal status. No matter who the citizens of the country vote for, members of the Electoral College can vote for anybody they want to (and as we shall see later, many have ignored the popular vote and done just that).

As a result of the Twelfth Amendment, in the presidential elections that followed, the members of the Electoral College chose presidents and vice presidents from the same party.

However, little else changed. It was still the Electoral College that chose the president and vice president, and five states still refused to allow the voters to have anything to do with choosing the electors.

Many of today's politician still do not want the people to be able to vote to elect the president directly. The reason is that whichever political party controls the smaller-population states still has much to gain by keeping the Electoral College system as it is.

Over the years, the Electoral College system has sometimes failed to agree with the people's choice for president. So why haven't the people risen up to demand an end to the Electoral College? Hard to say. It's probably just because we tend to forget about things if they seem to be working "all right." Only when things go wrong, do we get riled up and want to do something about it.

COMMENT:

The presidential elections of 1796 and 1800, the young nation's first nationally contested elections, revealed **the flaws in the Electoral College system**.

The most serious flaws are:

1. Electors are not chosen by the people. There is nothing in the Electoral College section of the Constitution that says the electors have to be guided by the popular vote for president and vice president. In fact, there is nothing in the Constitution at all about the need for a general election by the people. It simply says "the states" will select the electors.

2. Electors are not required to vote for the candidates chosen by the people. Under the Constitution, electors are not required to vote for the candidates chosen by the people's vote. That means electors can, and sometimes do, vote for their own preferred candidate instead of voting for the candidate preferred by the political party that named them as electors (see the later section on "faithless electors").

3. The current Electoral College winner-take-all system may influence how people vote. Because of the winner-take-all system, if the pre-election polls show that most of the voters in a state are clearly planning to vote for one candidate, there is little point for people to vote for a different candidate. That makes it less likely people will bother to vote at all. (Modern sophisticated polling methods have gotten much better at predicting which candidate will win a state.) If the polls show a lopsided victory is all but assured, **what is the point of anybody voting for either side?**

For example, in every election for the past sixty years (except for 1964 when Johnson won the national vote overwhelmingly), the

Republican candidate for president has won the winner-take-all electoral votes in Idaho, Montana, North Dakota, South Dakota, Utah, and Wyoming. So, with the polls already clearly showing that trend will continue in the 2012 presidential election, what is the point of anybody voting for president in those states? A vote for the Republican candidate is pointless because everybody knows the Republican always wins. And a vote for the Democratic candidate is also pointless because when the Electoral College meets to do the actual vote for president, under the winner-take-all system, **those votes will be thrown out.** It will be as if those people never voted at all.

4. A viable third party candidate can change the outcome. In the presidential election of 2000, most people believe third-party candidate Ralph Nader took enough votes away from Al Gore to cost him the presidency. Under the Electoral College system, it's surprising that hasn't happened more often.

5. A viable third party candidate could send the decision about who becomes president to the House of Representatives. According to the U.S. Constitution, a candidate has to get an **absolute majority** of all electoral votes to win the presidency. In a close election, if a third party candidate gets some Electoral College votes, it would make it hard for any candidate to get an absolute majority. In that case, the decision about who would be the president would go to the House of Representatives, and whichever party happens to be in the majority in the House at that time will undoubtedly determine which candidate gets to be president, no matter how the people voted. In the past, third party candidates have gained some Electoral College votes, but those elections were not close. It seems likely that sooner or later, a strong third party candidate will throw the election to the House of Representatives.

6. States with smaller populations have proportionally more electors than states with larger populations. Because even the smallest states are guaranteed under the Constitution to get at least three electoral votes, those states have a greater say in who will get to be president and vice president.

Because the design of the Electoral College gives more electoral voting power to the smaller-population states, a vote for president by a Wyoming resident counts about three times more than a vote by a California resident. That advantage was critical in the presidential election of 2000. In that election, **Al Gore won the 2000 presidential general election by 543,895 votes.** He did it by winning states with large populations, but the states with smaller populations, added together, had more Electoral College votes. As a result, Gore didn't get to be president despite winning the popular vote by a comfortable margin. It was the fourth time in U.S. history in which the candidate that won the popular vote didn't get to be president.

As you might expect, after the drawn-out battle in the House of Representatives with Burr refusing to cooperate, Aaron Burr was no longer looked on as favorably by the Democratic-Republicans. As a result, he was given little to do during his four-year rein as vice president.

When Jefferson ran for reelection in 1804, he dumped Burr in favor of New York Governor George Clinton.

The presidential campaign of 1800 saw, for the first time, **inflammatory, personal attacks** on the good names of the candidates. Personal attacks were not taken as lightly back then as they are now, and as a result, they **often resulted in duels.** After the 1800 election, a series of letters were circulated accusing Aaron Burr of various despicable acts. Thomas Jefferson, who was planning to run for reelection, replaced Burr with Governor **George Clinton** of New York to be his running mate.

As a result, Burr declared himself a candidate for governor of New York. Alexander Hamilton, the former Secretary of the Treasury, campaigned aggressively against Burr and Burr was defeated.

The insults continued even after the election until eventually, **Burr challenged Hamilton to a duel** and Hamilton accepted. On the morning of July 11, 1804, while Burr was still finishing out his term as vice president, the dueling parties were take by boat to New Jersey to avoid the anti-duel laws of New York state. There is disagreement about exactly what happened because everyone present was instructed to turn away before shots were fired (so they could not be brought into court to testify as to what happened). What is not in dispute is that Burr killed Hamilton with one shot.

Burr was never prosecuted for the killing.

Chapter Five
Presidential Politics Evolves

The Presidential Election of 1804

Although there was trouble brewing in Europe at the time of the presidential election of 1804, it was a period of relative peace in the United States. The American shipping trade had been further developed under President Jefferson, which resulted in an improved economy, and his successful negotiation and completion of the Louisiana Purchase was widely seen as a great achievement.

Therefore, Jefferson, with this new vice presidential candidate, George Clinton, was elected over **Charles Cotesworth Pinckney**, a Federalist from South Carolina.

COMMENT:

In 1803, President Thomas Jefferson initiated a deal with France to purchase a huge tract of land that became known as **the Louisiana Purchase**.

Jefferson was not sure at first whether or not he had the legal power to purchase land from a foreign government. However, he eventually decided it would be the best way to protect the port of New Orleans through which a great deal of the nation's farm produce passed.

Jefferson had previously served as Ambassador to France, and he had a tenuous working relationship with France. After Spain transferred *some* of the territory west of the Mississippi to France, Jefferson undertook to buy land from France in and around New Orleans.

Napoleon knew that his ongoing conflicts with Britain would eventually lead to war, so he needed all the money he could get. Therefore, he proposed to sell **all** of France's land west of the Mississippi to the United States for the total sum of 15 million dollars (about 3 cents an acre).

There was resistance in Congress over the deal, but the southern states favored it as long as Jefferson, a slave holder, agreed to allow the institution of slavery to expand into the new territory.

Eventually, the deal was made and the United States transferred three million in gold to France as a down payment and issued bonds for the other twelve million.

The U.S. assumed the new land stretched from the Gulf of Mexico in the south and into Canada to the north and all the way from the Mississippi River to the Rocky Mountains.

Spain disputed the sale and continued to claim the land.

When Jefferson funded the Lewis and Clark expedition to map the new territory, Spain sent troops to try to stop them. But they could never find the Lewis and Clark party.

Following river routes and being guided by friendly Indians, Lewis and Clark eventually made it all the way to the West Coast near what is now Portland, Oregon.

With the threat from Spain still looming, Jefferson established forts in several places to secure the new territory.

The new lands were to play a key role in three future conflicts, the Indian Wars, the War of 1812, and the Civil War.

The Presidential Election of 1808

In 1808, after the successful presidency of Thomas Jefferson, there was little doubt that his Secretary of State, James Madison, would be elected over Federalist Charles C. Pinckney who was running for president for the second time.

George Clinton was elected as his vice president. He was the first person to serve as vice president under two different presidents.

The Presidential Election of 1812

During the early part of the 19th century, the Democratic-Republican party was as dominant in U.S. politics as the Federalist had been in the first few presidential elections. And because the South continued to vote as a block, the Democratic-Republican presidential candidates were always slave holders from Virginia. With the support of *all* the southern states, they always won easily.

In the election of 1812, they nominated **James Madison** for reelection. He chose **Elbridge Gerry**, the former governor of Massachusetts as his running mate.

The Federalists, desperate for a win, supported a dissident Democratic-Republican, **DeWitt Clinton**.

The campaign election was, as usual, mostly about the issue of slavery, but this time there was also a war going on. Early in the election campaign, the United States declared war on Britain. It became known as the War of 1812.

The war was popular and as American have a history of reelecting presidents when a war is under way, they overwhelmingly voted to give Madison a second term.

COMMENT:

The war of 1812, like all wars, changed the political landscape and influenced several of the presidential elections that were to follow. The war started as an outgrowth (some said a sideshow) of ongoing battles between two great military powers of that era, Britain and France. Much of their war was being fought on the high seas, and when Britain tried to blockade France, trade ships from the United States sometimes got caught up in the conflict.

In the early 1800s Napoleon Bonaparte was running roughshod over Europe, but Britain ruled the seas. Britain put together an alliance of countries against Bonaparte's France, and in the early months of 1812, they began to capture American trade ships. Britain claimed the trade ships were helping the French, if only to re-supply France with needed goods. The American trade ships were taken as the spoils of war, and the captured sailors were forced to serve on British warships.

In response, on the first day of June in 1812, the United States shocked the world by declaring war on Britain. It was a reaction not only to the taking of American ships, but also a reaction to a perceived violation of America's neutrality in the European conflict. President Madison declared Britain's actions were an affront to America's honor.

Although America's declaration of war on Britain surprised many people throughout the world, the U.S. had some ongoing unsettled issues with Britain that played a part in it. For one thing, Britain had been trying to thwart the American expansion into American western territories the British wanted for themselves. They were arming the western Indians, trying to get them to organize against the United States.

In addition, there were many in the U.S. government that hoped not only to expand into the West, but also into Canada. Toward that end, one of the first American acts in the war was to invade Canada. American forces under General Hull, the governor of Michigan territory, invaded Canada north of Detroit. However, the attack was not well coordinated and the British not only easily repelled it, but in response attacked Detroit. Within a month, General Hull was forced to surrender Detroit to the British.

Several sea battles ensued, with American ships faring surprisingly well, but the land battles did not go so well. When De Witt Clinton, the governor of New York, sent troops into Canada near Niagara Falls, they were soon forced back and became trapped at the edge of the Niagara River with no way to cross back into the United States. Three hundred Americans were killed and nearly a thousand were taken prisoner.

Although the war wasn't going so well for the Americans, the people were mostly behind Madison and being patriotic in defiance of other, more powerful countries, was held in high regard. In fact, the American national anthem, **The Star-Spangled Banner,** was written during the war of 1812 (many Americans mistakenly believe it was written during the Revolutionary War).

The song's lyrics came from a poem titled "Defence of Fort McHenry" written by a 35-year-old lawyer named Francis Scott Key. He wrote the poem soon after he witnessed the British 25-hour bombardment of Fort McHenry, a large fort built in 1798 to defend Baltimore Harbor. At the time, the poem was sung to the tune of a British song written for a men's social club in London. With that tune more or less intact, it was named the national anthem 117 years later, in 1913.

In the War of 1812, even pirates played a role. Realizing that the U.S. was outmatched in naval power, the U.S. government offered to commission any armed vessel that was willing to help, even pirate vessels.

The famous pirate, Jean Lafitte, had been operating several smuggling ships out of New Orleans and had only recently been forced to retreat to an out-of-the-way bay further south.

A few months after the U.S. declared war on Britain, the British sent a delegation to try to recruit Lafitte to their side. They offered Lafitte and his men British citizenship and land in British areas of the western part of North America if they would fight against the Americans. Lafitte was a good enough tactician to see that the Americans held the land and therefore the advantage. He turned down the offer (and surprisingly didn't kill the envoys).

When the British mounted an offensive against New Orleans, Andrew Jackson brought troops to repel them.

The city was in dire straits and Jackson was outnumbered. He had only two ships and a few thousand unseasoned troops. When he learned Lafitte had many ships and seasoned fighting men, Jackson approached him with a deal: if the pirates would help defend the city, Jackson promised them full pardons. After the pirate agreed, Jackson managed to convince the Louisiana legislature to make the pardons official.

It is said that Lafitte's trained fighting men, and the pirates' knowledge of the area, were instrumental in the defense of the New Orleans. (By the way, just to make sure everyone knew he was still a pirate at heart, Lafitte went back to pirating after the war was over.)

After Napoleon's infamous failure to invade and hold Russia (he invaded Russia with 400,000 troops but came back with only 40,000), several countries united against France, and by 1814 Napoleon was defeated. Britain and France signed a peace treaty, and that put an end to the issues that had led to the War of 1812. The United States and Britain decided to call it a stalemate, and the two countries signed **the Treaty of Ghent** on the day before Christmas, 1814.

However, the treaty was signed in Europe, and as a result, the news that the war was over had to come to America by ship. And even after the news of the treaty had reached the East Coast, given the lack of rapid communications during that era, especially in the West, the news took over two months to reach all the troops that were still fighting. The last major battle of the war, a British victory at the second Battle of Fort Bowyer at Mobile Bay, Alabama, took place on February 11, 1815. Although the war was a stalemate with no territorial gains or losses, it did bring about a feeling of national pride and unity which resulted in a temporary **"era of good feelings"** in U.S. political matters. It also marked the beginning of an improving relationship with Britain.

The Presidential Election of 1816

By **1816**, the Federalists had all but given up hope. They didn't even nominate a candidate, and Democratic-Republican James Monroe, another Virginian, won easily. The only contention was whether the electoral votes of the new state of Indiana should be counted. For some reason, Representative John W. Taylor of New York objected to including Indiana's electoral votes. He was voted down and the votes of Indiana *were* counted (and it changed nothing).

The Presidential Election of 1820

By **the election of 1820**, the Federalist party was no more. Democratic-Republican **James Monroe ran for reelection unopposed.**

It would be the last time any candidate was to run for president unopposed.

After the War of 1812, politics in the early 1800s seemed relatively calm. There were ongoing troubles with the Indians as more and more western lands were developed, either pushing the Indians farther west or onto reservations.

In the West, continuing controversy over the issue of slavery was dividing the people. More and more people of the United States were saying slavery was not only inhuman, but it was also unconstitutional. America, they said, was supposed to be the land of the free, and yet slavery was still the law of the land in a time when many other countries were outlawing it.

France had abolished slavery until Napoleon brought it back temporarily by enslaving the citizens of the countries he invaded.

Countries such as Russia and other eastern European countries had abolished slavery many years before in the late 1700s.

Denmark and Norway abolished slavery and the slave trade.

In 1807, the British not only abolished slavery, but their ships began stopping slave ships and arresting their captains. It is estimated that the British anti-slave operation freed more than 150,000 captured Africans.

American's neighbors, Canada and Mexico had either abolished slavery or were in the process of doing it district by district.

The constant contention over the issue of slavery continued as the nation expanded westward. The southern states tried to enact laws that made slavery of African-Americans legal in any new western state that wanted to join the Union. The northern states fought against it.

The **Missouri Compromise** of 1821 maintained the balance of slave states and free states, which meant slavery would not be as big an issue in the upcoming elections as many had feared.

Chapter Six
The Politics of Slavery

Dissonance over the issue of slavery had been brewing in the United States since the country declared its independence from Britain. In the early 1800s, it became the predominant issue in presidential politics.

Many northerners were outraged at the very idea of slavery, saying it was contrary to the United States Bill of Rights. Those in favor of slavery pointed out that there was no mention of slavery in the U.S. Constitution (which is true; many of the framers of the Constitution, including George Washington, John Adams, Thomas Jefferson, and James Madison were slave owners and they were careful to never use the word "slave" anywhere in the Constitution).

Whenever new states petitioned to join the United States, it brought the issue to a head. The southern slave states feared if new states were allowed to join the Union as free states, the shift of power in Congress might lead to the eventual outlawing of slavery altogether. As a result, the slave states used their power in the Senate to keep new states from joining the Union unless they agreed to allow slavery.

The situation came to a head when Missouri wanted to join the United States. Missouri was the first state to be created out of the Louisiana purchase, and most of the region's citizens had come from the South. Therefore, there was an assumption that it would be a slave state. A House of Representatives committee approved Missouri's petition to become a state in 1819, but James Tallmadge of New York added an amendment specifying Missouri had to be a free state. Furthermore, his amendment stated that the new state would be prohibited from importing slaves and that all current slaves that had been born in the region had to be freed when they reached the age of 25. The bill was passed by the House on February 17, 1819.

Of course, the southern slave states used their disproportionate power in the Senate to vote it down.

After much contentious debate, as so often happens in politics, a compromise was reached and the bill was passed. The compromise was that the northern part of Massachusetts would break off to become a new state (Maine), and it would be admitted to the Union as a free state, and at the same time, Missouri would be admitted as a slave state. That way, there would be twelve slave states represented in the Senate which would make sure the twelve northern free states couldn't pass any anti-slave legislation. The law also included a stipulation that slavery should not be allowed in any territory north of latitude 36° 30' North (which marked the northern border of Missouri). The law became known as **the Missouri Compromise**.

As is typical of such compromises, neither side was happy with it. Thomas Jefferson said the division of the country created by **the Compromise Line** would eventually lead to the destruction of the Union. John Randolph, a Virginia slave owner himself, denounced the compromise and called Henry Clay, the Speaker of the House, "the great compromiser" (not a complimentary term). He sent plenty of other insults Clay's way, and not surprisingly, soon thereafter, the two met to fight a duel. Although shots reportedly were fired, the word from the dueling ground came back that the only injury was to Randolph's clothes (in other words, Clay did fire at Randolph, but it was a near miss).

Regardless of how Randolph felt about slavery, he felt all governing power should be in the hands of the states. He thought states ought to be free to accept or reject federal laws.

It is interesting to note that despite being a slave owner all his life, Randolph wrote a will that decreed all his slaves should be freed upon his death. Known as **manumission**, the practice of specifying the freeing of slaves in a will was becoming more common as the debate about slavery heated up, and Thomas Jefferson also specified in his will that his slaves be freed.

Later in life, Randolph said he regretted ever having owned slaves and his will provided money to be used to resettle his slaves in the free state of Ohio. After he died, three hundred and eighty three of Randolph's former slaves accepted the offer. However, at that time, racism was as rampant in Ohio as it was most everywhere else in this country, so when they arrived, they were met by mobs of angry white men with guns who drove them further on west. Sadly, the Ohio land that had been paid for with money from Randolph's will had already been sold off to white men, and the sellers had run off with the money. No Ohio law enforcement officials were willing to do anything about it, so all the "**Randolph slaves**" could do was move on. Eventually, many of them were employed by Quakers sympathetic to their plight, and the rest either found employment doing odd jobs in the few Ohio counties that would accept them, or else they moved on west and disappeared.

The Presidential Election of 1824

The presidential election of 1824 turned out to be as contentious as the battles in Congress over slavery. It was to be the **first election in which the candidate that won the most votes - both popular and in the Electoral College - did not get to be president.**

As I noted earlier, after the demise of the Federalist party, the Democratic-Republican Party much had things their own way. In every presidential election since 1796, the winner had been a member of the Democratic-Republican Party.

But by 1824, the people of the country were becoming disillusioned with the brand of "**insider politics**" that was becoming the norm, and that disillusionment was soon to have a devastating effect on the Democratic-Republican party's grip on political power.

Following the established precedent of serving only two terms, President Monroe chose not to run for reelection in 1824. He said he was ready to retire to his estate at Monroe Hill near Charlottesville, Virginia (his estate is now part of the campus of the University of Virginia).

As a result, **the 1824 election season** began, just as it had for all prior elections since the demise of the Federalist Party, with a **Democratic-Republican Congressional nominating caucus** (known then as the "**King Caucus**") being held to decide who would be the next president and vice president. For president, they selected a southern slave holder, **William Harris Crawford** of Georgia, and for vice president, they selected **Albert Gallatin** of Pennsylvania.

COMMENT:

The official **Democratic-Republican candidates, Crawford and Gallatin** were not well known at the time of their nomination. Nevertheless, both of them had been in and around politics for much of their adult lives.

In 1803, Crawford was elected to the Georgia House of Representatives, and in 1807 he was appointed to the U.S. Senate by the Georgia legislature (remember, until 1913, U.S. senators were not elected by the people but were appointed by state legislatures). In 1813, President James Madison had appointed Crawford to serve as minister to France. He served in that post until the end of the War of 1812, and when he returned from France, Madison appointed him Secretary of War, and then later Secretary of the Treasury. He remained in the latter position until, despite serious health problems, he was nominated to be a presidential candidate by the Democratic-Republican congressional caucus.

Albert Gallatin's story is a more complex and interesting one. Born into a wealthy and influential family in Switzerland, he studied at the elite Academy of Geneva where he discovered the philosophy of Jean-Jacques Rousseau and Physiocracy (the belief that the wealth of nations is based on the land and agriculture).

In 1780, at age 19, he began hearing about the democracy movement in the new country across the seas known as the United States. Like many other young Europeans, he was fascinated with the new democratic county and soon set out to see it for himself.

In America, he tried various business ventures without much success, so he had to make his living teaching French. Eventually, he was able to use his family's influence to get a position at Harvard College. That didn't last long. He again set out to make his fortune in various businesses from farming to retailing to glass making. At one point, in response to the perceived threat from France, the Commonwealth of Pennsylvania called out to its militia and Gallatin signed a contract to make muskets for them. That didn't turn out to be very profitable either.

But Gallatin had always had an interest in politics, and in 1793, he lobbied for an appointment to the U.S. Senate, aligning himself with the Democratic-Republicans and against the Federalists.

He was appointed to the Senate, but the Federalists protested his appointment, saying he had not been a citizen of the United States for a long enough period to be a senator.

It went to a vote, and the Federalists used their voting power to remove him from the Senate. But he did not go without at fight, and it was his battle to stay in the Senate and his impassioned oratory that brought him some attention, especially from the anti-Federalist forces. (One outcome of his battle to stay in the Senate was that the proceedings of the Senate, for the first time, had to be made public.)

Back home in Pennsylvania, he played a role in the Whiskey Rebellion, a protest against a new tax on whiskey that grew violent. When the government sent in the Army to put down the protest, Gallatin used his notoriety and his skillful oratory to calm the situation.

As a result, he was elected to House of Representatives in 1795 where he became an anti-Federalist leader of the Democratic-Republicans. From then on, he held various positions in the government until 1824 when he was nominated to be a candidate for vice president by the Democratic-Republican congressional caucus.

With the people crying out for more open politics, some politicians in the Democratic-Republican party saw opportunity. Many decided against participating in the "king making" party caucus. As a result, to the great surprise of the party leaders, only 66 of the party's 231 members showed up.

The caucus went ahead and nominated Crawford and Gallatin, but the lack of party participation was a sign of things to come.

Soon after the "official" Democratic-Republican caucus had nominated Crawford and Gallatin, three other Democratic-Republicans, **John Quincy Adams**, **Henry Clay**, and **Andrew Jackson** defied the party leaders and made it known *they* wanted to be president.

COMMENT:

The other Democratic-Republican candidates, John Quincy Adams, Henry Clay, and Andrew Jackson were better known. Adams was the son of the former president. Reportedly, he suffered from depression and was unsure of himself and not all that interested in politics. Nevertheless, he followed in his father's footsteps by serving as a foreign minister in several European countries.

Upon his return, he was still not sure he wanted to get involved in politics, but friends of his father pushed him in that direction. In 1802, he was elected to the Massachusetts State Senate.

That same year, he ran as the Federalist candidate for the United States House of Representatives, but he lost. Nevertheless, the Federalists soon got him appointed to the U.S. Senate where he served until 1808. As a senator, he angered the Federalists who had appointed him by supporting the Louisiana Purchase which they were against.

The Federalists, who controlled the Massachusetts legislature, decided to replace him. In response, Adams became a Democrat-Republican.

When James Madison, a Democratic-Republican, was elected president, he appointed Adams as foreign minister to Russia. He was accompanied in Saint Petersburg by his wife Louisa, and it was said at the time she made up for his lack of charm in social situations, and in fact, she soon became a favorite invitee at the tsar's parties.

By 1818, Adams was back in the U.S. serving as Secretary of State in the cabinet of Democratic-Republican President James Monroe.

With the election of 1824 drawing near, and it looking more and more like the election was going to be wide open, the New England Democratic-Republican party went looking for a "favorite son" candidate. Their choice fell to Adams, and eventually he was forced to accept their nomination.

Henry Clay was from a Virginian family who owned a large number of slaves. But Henry was not interested in the life of the plantation owner and instead decided to become a lawyer even though he had no formal education in the law. To learn about the law he secured an appointment as an assistant to the Virginia State Attorney where he learned about courtroom proceedings *and* about politics.

In 1797, he moved to Kentucky to practice law on his own. In Kentucky, everyone agreed he had a knack for politics and oratory, and in 1803, he was elected to the Kentucky General Assembly. It wasn't long before he was appointed by the Kentucky legislature to the U.S. Senate even though he was only 29 years old (the Constitution requires U.S. senators to be over the age of thirty). No one seemed to notice, or if they did, they didn't care.

In 1807, Clay returned to Kentucky where he was soon elected Speaker of the Kentucky House of Representatives.

However, his aggressive approach to lawmaking angered several members of the legislature, and he was involved in some scuffles on the floor of the House. One such scuffle resulted in Clay challenging a legislator named Humphrey Marshall to a duel. The rules of the duel were that each man would get three shots. One of Clay's shots grazed Marshall's chest, and one of Marshall's shots hit Clay in the thigh. Both men survived and honor was served.

In 1810, the Kentucky state legislature again appointed Clay to the U.S. Senate. But one year later, he was elected to the U.S. House of Representatives.

Such was his reputation that he was elected Speaker of the House on the first day in office. Thereafter, he was re-elected five times to the House and each time he was reelected as Speaker of the House. It is important to note that Clay completely changed the role of the Speaker of the House from parliamentarian (merely a keeper of the rules) to political leader. He was the first U.S. Speaker of the House to appoint his allies to key committee chairmanships as a way of controlling what became law and what did not. He also used his position to support hostilities against Britain which, in time, turned into the War of 1812.

By 1812, Clay was becoming quite prosperous and owned a 600-acre tobacco and hemp plantation and 60 slaves of his own.

In 1816, he became president of the **American Colonization Society**, a group that wanted to send free blacks back to Africa. Under Clay's leadership, the group founded a colony in Africa called Monrovia. Clay said the god of nature had decreed against the amalgamation of the black and white races as proven by the obvious differences of skin color and physical constitution. The main purpose of the group was to deport free blacks because they posed a threat to the practice of slavery, but some abolitionists from the North also got behind the effort.

As the election of 1824 loomed, it became clear the Democratic-Republican caucus's nomination of Crawford and Gallatin was not receiving wide support, and Clay made his bid for the presidency.

Andrew Jackson was the first candidate for president that could be described as `. Although he was, like Clay, a Southerner who owned slaves, he was not part of the Southeast Coast group of political insiders. He was from Tennessee.

Little is known about Jackson's childhood except that his father died before he was born, His father and his two brothers all died in the Revolutionary War.

When Jackson was thirteen, he joined up with a local militia to fight in the Revolutionary War. They made him a courier, but he was soon captured by the British and held as a prisoner of war. He was mistreated, almost starved to death, and contracted smallpox, leaving him with a lifelong hatred of the British. Soon after his release, his mother died, leaving him an orphan at the age of fourteen.

After that, he was bounced around between relatives, had little education, and worked at various odd jobs. Eventually, he went to North Carolina to study law. Not all that much is known about his studies or his early law career, but he was said to have practiced law in the western part of North Carolina, the area that was to become the state of Tennessee.

When Tennessee became a state in 1796, he was elected as its first representative in Congress. Meanwhile, he was growing wealthy from investments and from his law practice. He bought up huge tracks of land in Tennessee, and eventually accrued 150 slaves.

He also became an active member of the Tennessee militia. During the War of 1812, several Indian tribes banded together, and with the aid of the British, attacked western towns. Jackson took his Tennessee militia into battle against them, and the Indians were repelled. Jackson's rank was raised to major general, and he started to get a national reputation as a capable military leader.

In 1814, when New Orleans came under British attack, Jackson took over command of the region's defense. Many others came to join the defense effort, including Davy Crockett and Sam Houston, and by the beginning of 1815, the British were routed.

During that conflict, Jackson became widely known as a tough and very strict officer. The word got out that his men called him "Old Hickory" (tough as old hickory wood), and the nickname stuck.

By the end of the War of 1812, Jackson was being described as a national hero. He received an official gold medal of thanks from the U.S. Congress, and more than a few political leaders began thinking of him as a potential political candidate. In 1823, the Tennessee legislature appointed him U.S. senator and encouraged him to run for president in the presidential election of 1824.

As the 1824 campaign progressed, it started to become clear that William Crawford, the Democratic-Republican party's official choice for president, was not fairing well in the pubic eye. The campaigning had hardly begun when Crawford suffered a stroke that was said to have been brought on by an overdose of prescribed medication. He recovered well, but it hampered his ability to campaign and gave people doubts about his overall health.

It was only the first of many setbacks faced by the Democratic-Republican party leaders. Adams, the son of the nation's second president, who had formerly been a Federalist, was clearly gathering support from the old Federalists in the Northeast, and Jackson was beginning to look like the people's choice in the South and in the West.

Of the two, the party leaders thought Jackson would be the easiest to discredit. They published many articles in Democratic-Republican newspapers that said Jackson had **no real national political experience,** that he was **nothing but a frontier backwoodsman.**

But that didn't work very well because it made the people think of Jackson as "one of them."

Then the Adams backers **said Jackson was a murderer**. They said they had proof that he had executed captured Indians without a trial and had even executed captured British troops. There may have been some truth to those charges, but many people saw those incidents as just part of war, and Andrew Jackson had been, after all, a military hero in Florida and in the War of 1812.

As a last resort, Jackson's political opponents said he had killed men in unfair duels, and that he was an adulterer living with another man's wife.

Although there was some truth to those charges as well, Jackson's support among the "common men" in the West and the South never wavered. In that era, although adultery was a serious matter and did hurt Jackson's reputation, duels were seen as matter of honor between gentlemen.

COMMENT:

Although killing a man in a duel these days would certainly hurt a presidential candidate's chances of winning an election, it might well have been a political advantage in Jackson's time.

Jackson was rumored to have killed many men in duels, and it was a sign of the times that he never disputed the charge. His reputation of having great prowess with a pistol made a lot of the men of that era look up to him (and remember, at that time, only men could vote).

However, had the real truth about his dueling history been known at the time, it would have been considerably less flattering. While it was true that he was hot tempered and quick to challenge a man to a duel, the fact is his duels usually didn't take place. The problem was that he had a habit of challenging men to duels in the heat of the moment, only to find out later that his prospective opponent was a skillful and experienced duelist.

For example, at the tender age of 21, Jackson was trying to learn how to practice law. In one of his first court cases, an experienced lawyer ridiculed Jackson's judicial knowledge. Jackson immediately challenged the man to a duel. The duel was scheduled, but in the meantime, Jackson had learned more about the man's reputation as a duelist and had second thoughts. The details are lost to time, but the outcome on the field of honor was that both agreed to fire into the air.

Over the next several years, other duels were offered, but never took place. Not, that is until Jackson made an enemy of the governor of Tennessee, John Sevier. The story is that the two feuded for years until a duel was finally scheduled. However, before the day of the scheduled duel, they happened to meet on the trail. In a scene right out of one of that era's notorious western "dime novels," Jackson dismounted and pulled out his pistol. Sevier dismounted and drew his sword. Quite a few insults were exchanged before they both got back on their horses and went on their way. For some reason, the scheduled duel never happened.

The one duel that did happen, was indeed a deadly one. It was again a feud between lawyers, but it came to a head in a bar fight.

After the fisticuffs, Jackson challenged a young lawyer named Charles Dickinson to a duel. The duel took place at Harrison's Mill, Kentucky. Unfortunately for Jackson, the young man turned out to be quite a good marksman, and when the command to fire was given, the young man shot Jackson square in the chest. Jackson managed to stay on his feet and shot Dickinson in the stomach, killing him. Jackson survived, but he was to carry Dickinson's bullet in his chest for the rest of his life.

The attacks on John Quincy Adams by Jackson's supporters were quite different. They said Adams was out of touch with the people. They called him an **eastern elitist**, possibly, he was even a secret royalist. They constantly brought up Adams former involvement with the Federalists.

Those kinds of attacks were not likely to erode Adams's support in the Northeast and in the urban areas of the country, but they did hurt him with the voters Jackson was reaching out to, the so-called "common man" (and there were a lot more of them).

Meanwhile, one of the best known candidates for president, Henry Clay, was getting left behind. Although he was a well-known politician, it was clear he was not popular among the people. He could only count on his home state of Kentucky, and maybe some additional support from the two neighboring states.

Jackson won both the popular vote and the electoral vote. He racked up overwhelming victories in Alabama, Indiana, Mississippi, North Carolina, Pennsylvania, and Tennessee.

Adams won the popular vote in the Northeast states, Connecticut, Maine, Massachusetts, New Hampshire, and Rhode Island

The nation was divided by region: Jackson won the rural states by large margins, but Adams won the more populous states of the Northeast.

The only two states Crawford won were Delaware and Georgia. However, that doesn't mean Crawford was the people's choice in those two states. Delaware and Georgia did not allow a popular vote. The electors were chosen by the legislature. They were Democratic-Republican party loyalists who did their duty and cast their Electoral College votes for whoever the party leaders told them to - in this case, Crawford.

The final Electoral College vote was Jackson 99, Adams 84, Crawford 41, Clay 37.

Since no candidate had the required absolute majority of 131 electoral votes, the selection of the president would once again have to go to the U.S. House of Representatives. And as stated in the Twelfth Amendment, the House would have to choose from the top three candidates.

Interestingly, the vice president *was* elected. John Calhoun of South Carolina won the majority of votes for vice president and therefore was elected to that office no matter which of the presidential candidates won.

COMMENT:

Because **Henry Clay** had come in fourth in the Electoral College voting, he was eliminated from consideration. However, he was still the **Speaker of the House**, and that placed him in a position of great influence in the House.

At the time, Inauguration Day was in March. That meant the House would have to act quickly. But they didn't meet right away. First, there had to be the usual back room bargaining and arm-twisting. Some representatives were putting the word out that their votes could be "bought" in exchange for cabinet posts. Perhaps a vote could even be gotten with the promise of an important ambassador assignment.

Clay was the best at making such deals. He had been collecting political debts for many years, and now it was time to call them in. His main goal was to set himself up for the next presidential election. He knew Andrew Jackson, having won both the popular vote and the Electoral College vote, would be his main opposition in the next presidential election. Therefore, his goal was to manipulate the vote in the House to make sure Jackson didn't get to be president this time.

In those days, the usual stepping stone to the presidency was the cabinet position of Secretary of State. Many suspected Clay might try to accomplish his goals by working a deal with Adams. The deal would be that if Clay could convince enough representatives to vote against Jackson, Adams would be elected president, and in exchange, Adams would select Clay as his

Secretary of State. Clay believed that would put him in line for the presidency next time.

In actuality, Clay disliked Adams, but he thought he would have a better chance against Adams than Jackson in the next election.

As soon as the other representatives saw Clay meeting privately with Adams, they knew the deal was on.

Once the deal was made, it was Clay's job to get representatives to change their votes and go for Adams. It wasn't easy because few liked Adams. But with threats and promises, Clay was able to pull it off.

The House met to vote on February 9, 1825, and John Quincy Adams won the votes of 13 states, exactly the number needed to win the presidency.

Adams immediately named Clay as his Secretary of State.

Jackson and his supporters were furious. They called the deal Clay and Adams had made a "corrupt bargain." The term stuck, and in the end, undid all of Clay's attempts to set himself up for the presidency in the next election.

When the word of the House's vote and the "corrupt bargain" got out, the people who had voted for Jackson were outraged. They saw him as the rightful president-elect, and they could not be consoled by the politicians telling them that it had all been done according to the rule of law as specified by the Constitution's section on the Electoral College.

Jackson came right out and said the whole thing was a travesty. He and his supporters asked what kind of system it was where the person who won both the popular vote *and* the Electoral College vote did not get to be president. He said the rights of the people had been bartered away, and called for an immediate end to the Electoral College system of electing the president. He demanded to know why the nation's most important office should not be elected *directly by the people.*

Although just about everybody agreed that the corrupt deal method of selecting a president was not fair, the smaller-population states were completely united in their desire to keep the Electoral

College system. In the first place, the two extra electoral votes each of the smaller states got gave them an advantage in determining who the president would be. And they didn't want to change the system of letting the House of Representatives decide close elections, because if the House decided the presidency, every state got one vote, no matter how large or small the state was. That disproportionate advantage pretty much guaranteed Jackson's demand for an end to the Electoral College system would be ignored by the smaller states. And because such a change would require an amendment to the Constitution and ratification by three-fourths of states, even Jackson knew changing it would never happen.

The dissatisfaction with the results of the election of 1824 led to a significant change in the American political landscape. Jackson declared that he would run again in 1828, and because of the unfairness of how the 1824 election had turned out, many predicted he would win this time.

The senator from New York, Martin Van Buren, saw the people's anger at the way Jackson had been denied the presidency through back-room dealings as an opportunity to enhance his own fortunes. In the 1824 election, he had been a supporter of Crawford, but when it became clear that the people wanted the "outsider" Jackson instead of the usual Washington insider, he switched his allegiance and declared it was time for a new Jacksonian democracy. He said it would be a democracy of the common man instead of a political monopoly by the eastern elites (although he himself might accurately have been described as being part of that cadre).

Van Buren and Jackson broke with the all-powerful Democratic-Republican party. (Modern day Democrats now see that moment as the starting point of the Democratic party, and they claim Andrew Jackson as the party's founder.)

Leading up to the 1828 presidential election, the so-called **Jacksonian movement** gradually grew in political strength. It was a coalition of farmers and low-wage Irish-Catholic laborers. It was strongest in the states with the largest populations, which in those days included Virginia, New York, and Pennsylvania. This new **"democratic"** party was "for the people" and quite vocally against the "rich and the powerful."

In line with that belief, they fought to get rid of **voting rules** that said only men of property, or men who paid taxes, were allowed to vote. They said all white men should be allowed to vote. (It took many more years to accomplish that goal. By 1850, *nearly* all the "property requirements" had been eliminated in the *majority* of the states.)

The Jacksonian Democrats also believed America had a "**manifest destiny**" to expand throughout the American West, possibly all the way to the Pacific coast. However, they were against the expansion of slavery into the West.

The Jacksonians were against unlimited expansion of centralized federal power, but they could not be called states' righters because they believed the power should be in the hands of the people, not in the hands of the rich and powerful who normally ran politics. They strongly believed the Electoral College took power away from the people and put it into the hands of those rich and powerful politicians. They were also against the idea that it was the rich and powerful who appointed the members of United States Senate, but again there were frustrated by **the smaller-population states who didn't want the people to elect senators**. The South especially was against direct election of either presidents or senators because they were afraid the large states of the North would vote for men who might try to end slavery.

On the other hand, the Jacksonian democrats did generally favor a *laissez-faire* approach to economics; that is, they believed the federal government should not try to regulate businesses.

They also believed in a "**hard money system**" in which only gold and silver could be considered true currency. They were suspicious of banks, and were against the idea of a government bank.

The Jacksonian Democrats were in favor of the "**spoils system.**" The basic concept of the spoils system was that **to the victor shall go the spoils**; that is, a newly elected government official had the right to fire all of the previous administration's political appointees and bring in their own people.

COMMENT:

The Jacksonian Democrats' innovation of the **spoils system** is still in place today. Whenever a new president is elected, he gets rid of a large percentage of the former administration's top-level employees and surrounds himself with the party loyalists who helped get him elected. The reasoning of the Jacksonian Democrats was that only through the adoption of the spoils system could an administration be held accountable for their failures. It is the "buck stops here" concept, meaning the president makes all the personnel appointments; therefore he should be responsible for their failures. However, although modern day presidents still use the spoils system to replace many of the nation's top government officials as soon as they are elected, they now seem less willing to take the blame when things go wrong.

The Presidential Election of 1828

As a result of the national outrage over the fact that Andrew Jackson did not get to be president despite winning the vote in 1824 pretty much assured him the win in 1828. He and his running mate, John C. Calhoun from South Carolina, won easily. It would mark the beginning of an era of **"Jacksonian democracy"** that tried to take political power out of the hands of the rich and powerful "elitists."

COMMENT:

In response to Jackson's being elected president in 1828, Henry Clay and John Quincy Adams put together an oppositional coalition in Congress to fight against Jackson's new **Democratic Party**. Eventually, they took on the name **"Whigs."** (There was a Whig party in England that fought against the absolute rule of monarchy, and in America the term had been taken up as a reference to those who fought against tyranny.)

However, at first, the Whigs were not able to persuade the people that their plans for the nation were better than those of the

Democrats. For one thing, they were against the popular idea of westward expansion, insisting that modernization of the still-undeveloped nation in the East was more important. They felt Jackson and the Democrats were holding the nation back from modernization.

The Whigs *did* find support among the professional classes, business owners, and the owners of large plantations, but there were not enough voters in those groups to carry the next presidential election. When Clay ran for president as a Whig against Jackson in 1832, he got only 49 electoral votes as compared to Jackson's 219.

However, the Whig's plans to modernize the cities and the nation's manufacturers struck a chord in the cities that depended on manufacturing for their existence. As a result, the Whigs did win the vote in some cites even though the Democratic campaigns characterizing the Whigs as elites cost them a lot of votes among the poor.

The Democrats continued to describe the Whigs as the party of the rich and powerful, and that message resonated with the Irish-Catholic immigrants that had tended to settle in the eastern cities.

Some Protestant ministers, favoring the Whigs, tried to discredit the Irish-Catholics, telling their congregations that Jackson and his followers were immoral, and that a vote for the Democrats was a vote for immorality. Protestant reformers railed against drinking and whoring, and they proposed a national prohibition on sales of alcohol that would put and end to what they saw as "the liquor problem" in America.

Within a generation, the Whig Party was able to put up a candidate in nearly every election, and they gradually began to have more success.

The Whigs main agenda was to create an "**American system**" of rapid industrial growth and government support for manufacturers. They proposed high tariffs against foreign imports that might compete with American manufactured products. They were also in favor of government support of banking, and they felt the government should get involved in the expansion of the nation's infrastructure of roads and canals and railroads, anything that would make America more of a manufacturing country instead of an agrarian country.

The Whigs also felt America's educational system was in great need of modernization. They wanted the national government to get involved in creating a better public school system.

It soon became apparent that the main difference between the two political parties was that the Whigs felt the national government should be stronger and more involved in developing the future of the nation as a whole, while the Democrats felt such things should be left to the states.

The Presidential Election of 1832

The presidential election of 1832 saw the Democratic incumbent, **Andrew Jackson**, win easily against **Henry Clay** of Kentucky. Jackson won 219 of the 286 electoral votes cast. However, a number of other candidates also received electoral votes, mostly from their own states. They included John Floyd (who was not officially a candidate) who won 11 electoral votes, Hugh L. White who won 47 electoral votes, and Daniel Webster who won 23 electoral votes.

Jackson was reelected in 1832, and soon the outrage over the Electoral College was forgotten as new political parties were developed and new ideologies sprang up. For the next decade, the national political argument would be focused on concerns about slavery and about how involved the national government should be in people's lives.

The Presidential Election of 1836

The Democrats **held onto the presidency in 1836** when Jackson supported his vice president **Martin Van Buren** for president. Kentucky Senator **Richard Mentor Johnson** was chosen as Van Buren's running mate.

The Whigs, knowing they would have little chance against Jackson's Democrats, focused on electing members of the House of Representatives in case of an electoral deadlock which would again send the choice of a president to the House (where each state would get one vote).

COMMENT:

The selection of Richard Mentor Johnson as the Democratic vice presidential candidate in 1836 was surprising to many because he was known to be having a sexual relationship with one of his female slaves. He was quite open about it. Although it was well known that some slave owners had sex with their slaves, it was not seen as appropriate to discuss it openly.

Johnson's first sexual relationship was with a slave named Julia Chinn. He described her as his common law wife and admitted that he was the father of her two daughters.

When Julia Chinn died in 1833, Johnson started a new relationship with another female slave, but she left him for another man. Johnson sent his men to capture her, sold her at auction, and took up with her sister.

In political circles, there was much talk about Johnson's history of sex with his slaves, and even more talk about his unwillingness to keep quiet about it. As a result, when Van Buren ran for reelection in 1840, the Democratic party refused to endorse Johnson as his running mate. Nevertheless, Van Buren stuck with him.

Van Buren was defeated in his bid for reelection, and Johnson went back to Kentucky. In 1850, he was again elected to the to the Kentucky House of Representatives.

Johnson saw to it that both of Chinn's daughters were provided with an education and arranged for them both to marry white men.

Nevertheless, when Johnson died, the local judge ruled that he left no legal children and divided Johnson's considerable holdings between his brothers.

The Presidential Election of 1840

The **economic panic of 1837** had hurt the U.S. economy during Van Buren term in office. The people blamed the poor economy on the restrictive economic policies of **the Jacksonian Democrats**. As is common today, when the economy turns bad, the people vote against whatever political party is in power. That was the main reason why Van Buren's run for reelection failed.

In 1840, the Whigs put up **William H. Harrison** from Ohio He chose **John Tyler**, a U.S. Senator from Virginia.

Harrison was seen as a military hero for his role in victories against the Indians in the Northwest Indian War, and by campaigning against the economic policies of the Democrats, Harrison was able to defeat the incumbent president, Van Buren to **become the first Whig president**. However, Harrison died from pneumonia after only 32 days in office, and **Vice President Tyler** served out the rest of his term.

Although Tyler had been elected as a Whig, he disagreed with many of their proposals, and while he was still serving as president, he was thrown out of the Whig Party.

The Presidential Election of 1844

In the election of 1844, the issue of slavery became a major point of contention. **The Whigs again put up Clay, a slave owner**. Most of the Democrats wanted to nominate Van Buren again, but his stance against the expansion of slavery to new states meant the southern states would be unified against him.

After a contentious Democratic nominating convention, **James K. Polk**, a slave owner from Tennessee, emerged as the compromise candidate. He promised to serve only one term if elected and the Democrats decided to nominate him.

Polk won over Clay in a fairly close election, and was serving as president when statehood was granted to Texas, leading to **the Mexican-American War**.

COMMENT:

Unlike the War of 1812, the American people *were not* solidly behind **the Mexican-American War**. Democratic president Polk encouraged **the annexation of Texas** as part of his plan to expand the United States all the way to the Pacific Ocean even though it was almost sure to result in a war with Mexico. The Whig Party and anti-slavery groups were both against the annexation of Texas, and although their reasons for the opposition differed, it was one cause they were able to agree on.

In 1836, the Americans in the **Texas territory** had raised an army and had, after several bloody battles, defeated the troops of General Antonio López de Santa Anna, the dictator of Mexico. At the conclusion of that struggle, Texas declared itself to be an independent territory.

One of the main reasons the Texans had declared their independence from Mexico was that the Mexican government had tried to enforce its government policy forbidding the practice of slavery, and as soon as the declaration of Texan independence was official, many of the larger landholders began bringing in slaves from the American South to use in their farming and ranching enterprises. By 1845, slavery was a well-established practice in Texas, and that was the reason American anti-slavery groups were against granting Texas statehood.

Of course, the southern states were strongly in favor of granting Texas statehood, because it was a slave state. At that time, most of the territories petitioning for statehood were in the North and the southern states feared there would soon be enough non-slave states to outvote them in Congress. They knew that could mean the end of slavery in the United States.

Despite the anti-slavery protests and the opposition of the Whigs, in 1845, Texas' petition to become a state was granted.

At that time, Mexico was having its own internal battles, but they were united in their position that Texas still belonged to Mexico. As soon as Texas was granted statehood, Mexico said it would lead to war.

President Polk sent representatives to Mexico City to try to forestall hostilities, even offering Mexico huge amounts of money as compensation, but Mexico would not negotiate. They felt reclaiming what they saw as the theft of a piece of their country was a matter of national honor.

After the failure of negotiations, President Polk sent troops to establish a fort on the banks of the Rio Grande river. In response, Mexico sent 2,000 cavalry troops to the area. Accidentally, they ran into a small U.S. Army patrol and they killed 16 U.S. soldiers.

In response, President Polk declared, "Mexico has passed the boundary of the United States, has invaded our territory and shed American blood upon American soil." He demanded Congress grant a declaration of war against Mexico. After a short, but bitter, debate, they did so with the unanimous support of the southern Democrats.

Americans were divided over the war. Many in the North felt it was a war designed to spread slavery to the West.

Others, knowing that Mexico also controlled California, thought it might be a chance to grab California as well. There was also much talk about "manifest destiny" and the United States being from "sea to shining sea."

The Whigs, including Abraham Lincoln, continued to lobby against the war, the preparations for the coming battle went on unabated. Polk sent troops under the command of General Zachary Taylor into Mexico, and ordered naval forces to the Mexican coast in support.

At the same time, U.S. forces invaded California, and within a year, they controlled California from San Diego to San Francisco. On January 13, 1847, the **Treaty of Cahuenga** signifying the surrender of California was signed by the opposing military forces near what is now Los Angeles.

General Taylor went deeper into Mexico and General Santa Ana brought troops north from Mexico City to meet him. After extended fighting, Santa Ana was forced to retreat.

President Polk also sent a second army under General Winfield Scott to invade Mexico by sea. Santa Ana's army rallied to meet that advance, but was again routed.

Scott pushed on deeper into Mexico and soon captured Mexico City. Faced with the possible loss of even more territory, Mexico had no choice but to surrender. On February 2, 1848, Mexico signed **the Treaty of Guadalupe Hidalgo**, agreeing to the Texas boundaries specified by the United States.

Despite the relatively easy victory over Mexico, the people of the United States were still divided over the war and over the issue of slavery being expanded into the new western territories. It is worth noting here that President Ulysses S. Grant, who fought in Mexico under General Taylor, said in his later memoirs that the Civil War was largely the outgrowth of the Mexican-American war.

The Presidential Election of 1848

During the election of 1848, slavery was becoming an even more contentious issue than it had been in previous elections.

Zachary Taylor, a Virginia slave owner ran as a Whig and defeated **Lewis Cass** of Michigan in another close election, with each candidate carrying 15 states. If Cass had been able to carry New York, the Electoral College vote would have ended in a tie and the decision about who was president would have again been sent to the House of Representatives.

The Presidential Election of 1852

In **the election of 1852**, the Democratic presidential nominating convention at first got nowhere because of constant arguing about how to deal with the issue of slavery. When they finally did get around to the nominations, there were four strong candidates and therefore the voting got nowhere. Finally, **Franklin Pierce**, who was not one of the four main candidates, was put up as a compromise candidate and eventually was selected. Pierce was from the small state of New Hampshire, a non-slave state. However, he was known to favor allowing slavery to be practiced in the new western states. His main attribute as far as the Democrats were concerned was that he had fought in the Mexican-American War and had been so valued as a leader of men that he had risen to the rank of brigadier general of volunteers.

The Whigs nominating convention also had to deal with agitation over the slavery issue, but in the end, the party leaders decided to support the **Compromise of 1850,** which was a compromise that forced Texas to surrendered its claim to New Mexico, and allowed California to come in as a free state. However, the South added language to the compromise that allowed new states to decide for themselves whether to allow slavery or not. That overturned the prior **Missouri Compromise** of 1821 which made slavery illegal north of the **Compromise Line** (any territory north of latitude 36° 30′ North which marked the northern border of Missouri). The South was also able to insert the **Fugitive Slave Act** into the compromise which made it illegal for slaves to run away to the north and specified that if they did, the North had to return them to their rightful owners.

After much contention, the Whigs finally nominated **Winfield Scott**, another Virginian from a slave-holding family who had made his name as a general in the Mexican-American war. Although his family still owned many slaves, he made it known that he was against expanding slavery to the West.

The issue of slavery was to play a big part in the presidential election of 1852. People were note sure of the Whig position on slavery. Scott was a slave owner, but he said he was against expanding slavery into the new western states. Because Scott's stated position on slavery was not in line with the wishes of the southern states, he did not get the solid support from southern voters he expected, and as a result, Pierce, a relative unknown, won the election.

COMMENT:

Most people thought **General Winfield Scott** would be elected president simply because he was **a military hero** in the Mexican-American War and in the Indian Wars.

However, the Mexican-American War was not fully supported by most Americans because of the slavery issue in Texas. And there were rumors that his **"victories" over the Indians** included almost-unbelievable **cruelty to non-combatant Native Americans.**

Although most Americans supported the idea of moving the Indians off their land and onto reservations, the citizens of the East did not support excessive cruelty while doing it. News about the terrible treatment of the Indians leaked out, diminishing Scott's reputation as a military hero.

However, in Scott's defense, it should be pointed out that he was just carrying out policies that had been around for a long time. A policy of "civilizing" American Indians had been in place since the presidency of George Washington. Under Washington, Indian agents were assigned to make the Indians give up their nomadic hunting and gathering ways and force them to settle down to farming.

They Indian tribes were also encouraged to break up the communal lands and assign property ownership the individual Indian families. The problem was, as soon as that was done, the land could be sold, and through various means, some legal and some not so legal means, much of what had been Indian lands ended up in the hands of white settlers.

Many Indian tribes, including the Cherokee, Chickasaw, Choctaw, Creek, and Seminole, resisted resettlement, so Congress passed the **Indian Removal Act**. President Jackson signed it into law at the beginning of the summer of 1830. It was deemed that the tribes would resettle to unclaimed land far to the west, into what is now Oklahoma, an area that was henceforth deemed to be "Indian lands."

By law, communal Indian lands were considered sovereign. That meant they were not under the control of the United States, and therefore could only be acquired by the United States through treaties. However, pursuant to the Indian Removal Act, the Indians were put into a position of either signing treaties that would give them *some* payment for their lands and the right to settle in new land in the West, or face the prospect of being forcibly removed and getting nothing. Many signed, but many others refused to leave their ancestral lands. Some used the services of sympathetic lawyers to try to fight the act, but had little success. A key 1823 Supreme Court decision stated that Indians could only *occupy* land within the United States; they could not legally hold title to those lands.

In 1838, General Scott was sent to forcibly move the Indians off their lands and into holding camps. General Scott wanted to use regular troops to do the job, hoping they would treat the Indians more humanely than the locals, but none were available, so he had to use the local militia. Almost all of the 7,000 militiamen that participated were local citizens who were glad to get rid of the Indians so they could take over their lands.

By the time it was over, the newspapers were proudly reporting that Scott's troops had captured or killed every Indian in Alabama, Georgia, North Carolina, and Tennessee. Those that were captured were sent to concentration camps near the U.S. Indian Agency near Cleveland, Tennessee. Then, they were sent West.

In the dead of winter of 1838, most of the remaining Native Americans, including almost all of the 15,000 Indians that were part of the Cherokee nation, were forced to walk one thousand miles west to the new reservations. Most had little warm clothing and some were barefoot. Many had contracted smallpox while being held in the concentration camps, and as a result, untold thousands died on the trail. It became known as the **Trail of Tears**.

The Presidential Election of 1856

By the time the election of 1856 came around, the Whig Party had been torn apart by the issue of slavery.

A new party, **the Republican Party**, emerged specifically to fight the spread of slavery to new states entering the Union.

The **Kansas Nebraska Act** of 1854 had created the new territories of Kansas and Nebraska, but the South had again used its unfair voting advantage in Congress to force language to be inserted into the law to allow the new states to determine for themselves whether or not to allow slavery. Once again, they ignored the previous compromise, known as **the Missouri Compromise,** which made slavery illegal north of Missouri.

President Pierce's handling of the contention over slavery in Kansas proved to be his undoing. His party, sensing defeat at the polls, refused to grant his request to be nominated for a second term. Instead, they nominated **John C. Fremont**, another Mexican-American war hero from the new state of California.

COMMENT:

The result of the **Kansas Nebraska Act** was immediate contention over the issue of slavery in the new states, especially in Kansas. Slave holders in Missouri flooded across the border into Kansas and created a territorial legislature in a town near the Missouri border. One of their first acts was to pass a law making Kansas a slave state.

In response, a "**free soil**" group set up an opposing legislature in Topeka. They declared the slave holder's legislation invalid. The "free soil" advocates opposed what they called "**slave power.**" Slave power was the idea that the southern slave states had so much inordinate power in Congress and in electing the president, they would be able to move into any new state and establish it as a slave state. Then they would buy up all the land, and bring in slaves.

Tensions escalated when an armed group of pro-slavery men attacked the free-state town of Lawrence Kansas to destroy the anti-slavery newspaper offices. They burned buildings and stole everything they could get their hands on from the homes of the citizens.

Senator Charles Sumner of Massachusetts denounced the attacks in Kansas, and in response, Preston Smith Brooks, a congressman from South Carolina came into the Senate chambers and attacked Sumner with a cane. The senators who were present tried to stop the attack, but some of the southern representatives pulled out pistols and held them back to let the attack go on. Sumner was beaten so badly he was bedridden for years and was unable to return to the Senate.

Soon, John Brown, a well-known anti-slavery advocate, went to Kansas and entered the fray. One of his first acts was to lead an attack on a pro-slavery settlement at Pottawatomie Creek where he and his supporters killed five men.

As the tensions escalated, Congress passed a resolution declaring the pro-slavery legislature illegal in Kansas and the resolutions they had passed as improperly done.

But President Pierce ignored the congressional resolution and continued to recognize the pro-slavery legislature. Then he outraged the North by sending federal troops to break up the anti-slavery legislature.

Emboldened by the support of the president, Missouri pro-slavery men formed an army and marched into Kansas.

In what was to become known as the time of **Bleeding Kansas**, battles between the pro-slavery forces and the anti-slavery forces continued for years, foreshadowing the terrible Civil War that was to come.

When the American Civil War did finally break out a few years later, Kansas continued to be a battleground between North and South.

In opposition to **John C. Fremont**, the Whig's candidate in the 1856 election, the Democrats nominated Senator **James Buchanan** from Pennsylvania. Buchanan won the election, however, the relatively unknown Fremont had managed to carry 33% of the popular vote, which is remarkable given that he got **no votes at all in the South**. This established the Republican Party as a viable political force in the United States.

Chapter Seven
The Election of Lincoln and a Country in Crisis

The Presidential Election of 1860

The presidential election of 1860 was the most contentious election in the history of the nation, and it led directly to the Civil War. The contention about slavery that had divided the nation for so long, was about to break out in armed conflict.

Throughout the history of the United States, **the South had tried to maintain enough of a voting advantage in Congress** to block new free states from joining the Union. Most other nations had already outlawed slavery, so the South knew that if they allowed a majority of even one free state to exist in Congress, the voting power of the North would make it likely that sooner or later Congress would vote to outlaw slavery.

The South's control of Congress and the Electoral College went all the way back to the founding of the nation when they had refused to join the Union unless they got extra power in both Congress and the election of presidents. Eight of the original thirteen states, Delaware, New Jersey, Georgia, New York, Maryland, South Carolina, Virginia, and North Carolina allowed slavery, and they always voted as a block.

However, as the nation grew in the mid-1800s, more free states joined the Union. Up until then, the South had managed to use their veto power in Congress to maintain the balance between slave states and free states. By 1848, there were fifteen slave states, Delaware, Georgia, Maryland, South Carolina, Virginia, North Carolina, Kentucky, Tennessee, Louisiana, Mississippi, Alabama, Missouri, Arkansas, Florida, and Texas. There were fifteen free states, New Jersey, Pennsylvania, Connecticut, Massachusetts, New Hampshire, New York, Rhode Island, Vermont, Ohio, Indiana, Illinois, Maine, Michigan, Iowa, and Wisconsin. But as a result of the Mexican-

American War, in 1850, California was brought in as a free state and that upset the balance.

Soon, other western states petitioned to join the Union. As we have seen, the Kansas Nebraska Act of 1854 made it possible that these new states could become slave states, and the Republican Party was formed to fight against that possibility.

In 1856, to make their point, the Republicans had nominated **John C. Fremont** for president simply because he was from the new free state of California. When two more western states, **Minnesota and Oregon, joined the Union** in 1858 and 1859, they also chose not to become slave states.

For the South, the handwriting was on the wall. They had lost their voting advantage in both the Senate and in the Electoral College, and it was clear that sooner or later, the northern states would elect a president that would lead to an effort to abolish slavery.

That was the situation leading into the presidential election of 1860. It was clear that slavery would be the main issue in the election, and the issue was sending the American political situation into chaos. New political movements were springing up as special-interest groups fought to gain control over both local and national political interests.

The Democrats held their 1860 presidential nominating convention in Charleston, South Carolina, which assured that there would be plenty of agitation from the local pro-slavery groups.

Senator Stephen A. Douglas was from the free state of Illinois, but he had been a key proponent of the Kansas Nebraska Act which allowed states to decide for themselves whether to allow slavery or not, so many in the party thought he would make a good compromise candidate. He had made a name for himself as a capable orator in his campaign against **Abraham Lincoln** for an Illinois Senate seat.

But the Democratic Party was deeply divided. The **Supreme Court's Dred Scott decision** of 1857 had shocked the nation by declaring that the Constitution protected slavery in the United States, and the party leaders knew that the nation's voters would be paying as much attention to the party's stance on slavery as to what candidate they nominated.

Many southern hard liners insisted the Democratic party should openly take a pro-slavery stance and try to elect a president that would fight for legislation to make slavery legal in all states. But now that the South had lost their advantage in the Electoral College, the party leaders knew that would all but guarantee a loss in the upcoming election.

By the time balloting began, six major candidates had been put forward for the Democratic nomination. In the first ballot, Douglas led, but by not enough to be the nominee. There were just too many staunch pro-slavery delegates against him. The balloting went on and on with much pro-slavery agitation until finally, after 57 ballots, the delegates voted to adjourn the convention and meet again later in a northern city.

By the time the Democrats met again two months later in Baltimore, there was contention as to whether the troublesome pro-slavery delegates from the South should even be admitted. In the heated debate that resulted, all of the southern delegates walked out, thus assuring Douglas's nomination. As a compromise, Senator Benjamin Fitzpatrick of Alabama was nominated for vice president, but he refused to run with Douglas and was replaced by former Senator Herschel V. Johnson of Georgia.

The Southern delegates who had walked out held their own convention and nominated John C. Breckinridge from Kentucky for president and Joseph Lane from North Carolina for vice president.

COMMENT:

The Supreme Court's Dred Scott decision of 1857 caused an uproar throughout the North. The court had been asked to decide if Dred Scott, a slave who been taken by his master to the free state of Illinois was free or still a slave. He had been legally married while in Illinois, even though slaves were not supposed to have any legal rights, including the right to marry. The court, in a seven to two decision, shocked the northern free states by stating that slaves were not legal citizens of the United States and therefore had no legal right to appeal to the court. The majority members of the Supreme Court went on to state that slaves were private property even if they were taken to a free state. They said a slave could not be taken away from his or her owner without due process.

> Unexpectedly, the court's decision triggered the economic panic of 1857 when investors, anticipating trouble, suddenly lost faith in their investments.

The 1860 Republican presidential nominating convention was held in Chicago a month after the debacle of the Democrat's convention in South Carolina.

The favorite candidate going into the Republican convention was former New York Governor William H. Seward, and he led after the first two ballots. But when he failed to rally any more delegates to his side, a local Illinois dark horse, Abraham Lincoln, was nominated. He had gained some national notoriety as a calm and effective orator in his series of debates with Stephen Douglas during their race for an Illinois Senate seat. Of special note was the Republican Party's written platform: it stated that slavery would not be allowed to spread any further.

The 1860 presidential election ballots included the following candidates: **Abraham Lincoln**, Republican; **Stephen Douglas**, Democrat; **John Breckenridge**, Southern Democrat; **John Bell**, Constitutional Union. The result was that the southern votes were split between Breckenridge, Bell, and Douglas, leading to a relatively easy victory for Lincoln.

Immediately after Lincoln's election, seven southern states, South Carolina, Mississippi, Florida, Alabama, Georgia, Louisiana, and Texas **seceded from the Union**. When hostilities commenced with the Confederate forces attacking Fort Sumter in South Carolina on April 12, 1861, four additional states, Virginia, Arkansas, North Carolina, and Tennessee joined the Confederacy.

COMMENT:

The causes and effects of the **American Civil War** are beyond the scope of a book about the Electoral College and how U.S. presidents are elected. Thousands of other books have discussed the Civil War, and its causes and consequences have been covered in great detail.

But I should point out that it was the biased Electoral College system, along with the two votes each southern state got in the U.S. Senate, plus the extra votes the South got in the House of Representatives by the counting of millions of slaves as part of their population, that kept the South in the Union as long as it did. The South's extra voting power in the Electoral College resulted in ten of the first twelve presidents being southern slave holders, and they made sure slavery continued to be the law of the land.

Even after northerners began to be elected president, the South was able to use their voting power to keep a balance between slave states and free states. That ended up making the United States the last major country in the world to abolish slavery.

As soon as the Civil War started, President Lincoln took a hands-on approach. He personally supervised the North's war strategy and selected the generals to fight it. And when he was disappointed with the performances of his generals, he replaced them. Eventually, Lincoln selected General **Ulysses S. Grant,** a military leader who was having great success in the West. Lincoln called him to Washington and named him to be his top general.

Lincoln knew he was going to have to try to hold the nation together throughout a war that would pit friends and family against each other, but he also wanted to live up to his promise to end slavery. During his first term in office, he announced the Emancipation Proclamation, and urged Congress to pass an amendment to the Constitution outlawing slavery.

He appointed five judges to the Supreme Court, all of them well known for their anti-slavery positions. But he did not want the nation to be forever divided, so long before the war ended, he was already proposing plans for the reconstruction of the South.

The Presidential Election of 1864

Despite the terrible loss of human life in the war, Lincoln was again nominated by the Republicans for reelection in 1864.

However, Lincoln was unhappy with his vice president, Hannibal Hamlin. He replaced him with Andrew Johnson. It was a decision that was to have a profound effect on Johnson's life.

The Democrats put up General **George B. McClellan**, the general Lincoln had demoted early in the war.

McClellen won only a few states. Lincoln won reelection, and because there was no southern vote, it was an easy victory.

In the days after Lincoln's reelection, the war dragged on into yet another spring. However, Lincoln was sure the war would soon be over. The Confederate Army was exhausted and in retreat, but the southern leadership was still not ready to give in.

The Union Army marched deeper into the southern states, freeing millions of slaves as they went. At Lincoln's request, some of the slaves were recruited into black regiments of the Union Army.

Extended Union Army forays into the South, such as Sherman's infamous **March to the Sea,** destroyed much of the South's ability to continue the war.

Lee understood that continuing to fight would only result in more pointless bloodshed He finally surrendered his army to General Grant at Appomattox, Virginia on April 9, 1865.

A week later, even as the nation continued to celebrate the end of long and terrible war, Lincoln was assassinated by **John Wilkes Booth**, a well-known actor who was secretly a spy being supported by the Confederate secret service

Lincoln's vice president, **Andrew Johnson**, was sworn in as president the next morning, and for the next four years, he oversaw the rebuilding of the nation. He was known as a compromiser who repeatedly vetoed Congressional bills that were designed to punish the South or to give more rights to the freed slaves.

When Congress passed a bill to create the Fourteenth Amendment, he vetoed it. The amendment provided civil rights to all U.S. citizens, including freed slaves, and included an Equal Protection Clause that *required* each state to provide equal protection under the law to *all* people within its jurisdiction.

Congress quickly overrode Johnson's veto, and there was a move to impeach him. The vote in the House of Representatives to remove Johnson from office failed by only one vote.

Chapter Eight
Democrats Versus Republicans

The Presidential Election of 1868

Shunned by the Republican Party, for the election of 1868, Johnson sought reelection support from the Democrats. But they didn't want him either. Instead, they nominated Horatio Seymour, the former governor of New York.

The Republicans quickly nominated war hero, General Ulysses S. Grant who won both the general election and the Electoral College vote.

However, Seymour, the Democratic nominee, shocked the nation by winning his home state of New York, and it was said if southern voters would have been allowed to vote in 1868, the outcome of the election would have been quite different. An accusation of voter fraud in New York was put forth and a Congressional investigation was initiated, but in the end, no action was taken.

The Presidential Election of 1872

In the presidential election of 1872, Grant easily won reelection, but five other candidates also won Electoral College votes. New York newspaper owner, Horace Greeley, came in second in the popular vote, but died before the Electoral College met. (Despite his not being alive, three electors voted for him anyhow).

The electoral votes from five southern state were questioned, and the electoral votes of Arkansas and Louisiana were rejected due to clear evidence of voter fraud and intimidation of African-American voters.

The Presidential Election of 1876

The election of 1876 was one of the most controversial in the history of the United States.

For president, the Republicans nominated **Rutherford B. Hayes**, the former governor of Ohio. He chose as his vice president, **William Wheeler**, a U.S. Representative from New York.

Hayes was a compromise candidate, selected after many ballots at the Republican nominating convention failed to produce a clear winner.

The Democrats nominated **New York Governor Samuel J. Tilden**. Tilden had gained national recognition for managing to finally send New York's corrupt Boss Tweed to prison.

COMMENT:

Politics during the nineteenth century was a rough and tumble business. Although some may say politics in our current era is mostly run by the rich, it was clearly so in New York in the mid 1800s.

William Tweed, known as "**Boss Tweed**," was one of the largest landowners in the state of New York, and he was a director of railroads and banks. He was elected to Congress in 1852 and later served in the New York state Senate.

After that, he got himself appointed to various city positions in which he could dispense political favors - for a price. By controlling New York City boards and commissions, he was able to gain great influence over local politics, and even more influence over how public money was spent. Over time, he was able to create a political machine that controlled much of New York's politics. He became known as the "Grand Sachem" of Tammany Hall.

The end of his "reign" came when Governor Tilden worked with local prosecutors to convict him of stealing millions of dollars of public money through various schemes. The prosecution said he paid "workers" huge payments for mostly nonexistent city building projects just to get kickbacks. They gave examples such as the plasterer who had been paid over a hundred thousand dollars for a day's work and a carpenter who had been paid over three hundred thousand dollars for doing woodwork carpentry in a building that turned out not to have any woodwork in it (this in era during which the average urban New England worker made about $300 **per year**).

Tweed was imprisoned, and a million dollar bail was set. He had no trouble raising that much money and was therefore released.

Unbelievably, while all this was going on, Tweed was re-elected to the state senate.

But soon, he was arrested again, and this time the bail was raised to eight million dollars, an astounding amount of money in that era. Again, he had no trouble raising it.

But it was clear his empire was falling apart. His associates were also being arrested, and some of them were being convicted despite Tweed's attempts to subvert the legal process.

Tweed was finally convicted of corruption and graft and given a prison sentence of twelve years. But when the local jailers allowed him out for a "home visit," he escaped and fled to Spain. He was eventually caught there and put on an American warship to be brought back to the United States.

Now apparently out of money and desperate to get out of prison, he said he would tell prosecutors all about how his corruption system worked if they would release him. An agreement was reached that resulted in the prosecution of many members of his inner ring.

After confessing, Tweed was ready to get out of prison so he could to try to reestablish his empire. But Governor Tilden refused to let him go. Tweed was held in a local New York City jail until his death in 1878.

Everyone knew the election of 1876 was going to be close. The Democrats were resurgent, especially in the South, and with the retirement of General Grant, they felt they had a good chance to take the presidency back from the Republicans. The Democrats tried to paint the Republicans as involved in graft and political manipulation, and contrasted them with Tilden who had a reputation as a reformer.

The Republicans main approach to the campaign was to remind the people that it was the Democrats that had caused the Civil War through their support of slavery.

The Democrats referred to this tactic as "waving the bloody shirt," and pointed out that not every Democrat had been a rebel. They reminded the voters that both Tilden and his running mate, **Thomas Hendricks**, were Northerners. They called for **an end to reconstruction** and a return to normalcy. It was a message that appealed to a war-exhausted country.

During the election, southern paramilitary groups such as the **Red Shirts** and the **White League** disrupted Republican rallies and used violence and intimidation to try to stop Republicans, and especially blacks, from voting.

When the results of the popular vote were in, Tilden, the choice of the southern states, had won by 252,666 votes, the closest national vote in history.

However, there were cries of fraud with regard to the counting of votes in the South. The Republicans claimed their voters in Florida had either not been allowed to vote or had been tricked into voting for the wrong candidate by deceptively designed ballots. They cited numerous instances of voter intimidation and fraud in Florida, pointing out that documents certifying the election there had been signed by the state attorney-general, a Democratic, and by the Florida governor, also a Democrat (as we shall see in a later chapter, Al Gore's supporters were later to make similar accusations regarding the 2000 election in Florida).

Reports of voter intimidation and ballot fraud were also raised in Louisiana, and South Carolina. One of the Democratic tricks in the South was to print a picture of Abraham Lincoln on the Democratic ballot to try to get illiterate voters to select that one.

In addition, because the Constitution did not stipulate that Electoral College electors *had to* vote for the popular vote winner, there was no assurance that southern Democratic electors would be willing to cast their votes for the anti-slavery Republicans.

When the ballots of the Electoral College voters were counted, it appeared that Hayes had won by one vote. But neither candidate had the requisite 185 electoral votes that were required for a majority. It appeared that once again the selection of the president would be done in the House of Representatives (at that time, the House was controlled by the Republicans).

Because of the many accusations of voter fraud in the South, Congress created a special commission to review the results. All that did was lead to more contention about who should be appointed to the special commission. In the end, the Democrats (who controlled the Senate because of the two senators given to each southern state) were allowed to appoint five members, and the Republicans (who controlled the population-based House of Representatives) were also allowed to appoint five. Four Supreme Court justices were added to the commission, two with Republican leanings, and two with Democratic leanings. Those four Supreme Court justices were allowed to select one more justice to serve on the committee, and they chose Justice David Davis who they saw as politically independent. Hoping to gain a deciding vote on the committee, the Democratically-controlled Illinois senate immediately appointed Davis to fill their vacant U.S. Senate seat. But their plan backfired when Davis resigned from the Supreme Court to become a senator. The four justices selected Justice Joseph P. Bradley who was supposed to be another impartial member of the court.

In January of 1877, the special Congressional committee met to examine the results of the Electoral College votes from Florida, Louisiana, Oregon, and South Carolina. If the committee hoped for easy answers, they were disappointed: those states each presented two conflicting sets of Electoral College results, one from the Republicans and one from the Democrats.

After much debate, the Congressional members of the committee voted right along party lines. That meant the vote was a tie. The decision was up to Justice Bradley. He voted with the Republicans, making the decision 8-7 in favor of giving the disputed Electoral College votes to Hayes. That gave Hayes a 185-184 Electoral College victory.

The election of 1876 is the only election in the history of the United States in which a candidate **received an absolute majority of the popular vote and did not get to be president** (although Al Gore won the popular vote in the 2000 election by 543,895 votes, because a third-party candidate also received votes, Gore did not win an absolute majority).

It is not clear under what authority Congress made their decision because there is nothing in the Constitution that allows the winner of the Electoral College to be denied the presidency. Most people in the South thought the election had been stolen from Tilden by the North, but the people of the North felt that Hayes would have won if the many former slaves in the South had been allowed to vote.

The Presidential Election of 1880

In the 1880 presidential election, the popular vote was extremely close with **James Garfield**, a Republican from Ohio, getting 4,453,337 votes to Democrat **Winfield Scott Hancock**'s 4,444,267 votes. With a tiny national margin of only 9,070 votes, you would expect the Electoral College to end in a tie. But because of the strange winner-take-all system which had by then been accepted by almost every state, Garfield won by 214 to 155. To understand how that could happen, we have to look at the state-by-state results.

Of course, Garfield, the Republican, won all the northern states, and Hancock, the Democrat, won all the southern states. However, now that there were more northern states in the Union, they had enough Electoral College votes to give Garfield the victory.

Interestingly, if only a few thousand voters in a handful of northern states had voted for Hancock, he would have won both the popular vote and the Electoral College vote. Garfield was assassinated during his first year in office and his vice president, **Chester A. Arthur** served out the remainder of his term.

The Presidential Election of 1884

In the presidential election of 1884, a Democrat won for the first time in 28 years. After Republican **Chester Arthur** declined to run for reelection due to health problems, Democrat **Grover Cleveland** ran against Republican **James G. Blaine** from Maine. Cleveland won the national popular vote by a very narrow 57,579 margin, and by 219 to 182 in the Electoral College. He did it by winning the southern states, and by winning Indiana, New Jersey, and most importantly New York. He won the popular vote in New York by only 1,149 votes, thereby gaining **all** of New York's 36 electoral votes. Had those 1,149 votes gone the other way, Cleveland would have still won the national popular vote, but Blaine would have been elected the nation's 20th president in the Electoral College.

The Presidential Election of 1888

In the presidential election of 1888, Democrat **Grover Cleveland** ran for reelection and won the popular vote. However, Republican **Benjamin Harrison** from Indiana got more Electoral College votes and was therefore elected president.

In the nationwide popular vote, Harrison got 5,443,633 to Cleveland's 5,538,163. Cleveland had won by 94,530 votes. So why wasn't he elected president? Once again, it was the strange workings of the Electoral College that determined who would be president, not the will of the people.

The reason Harrison won the Electoral College vote was because he was able to squeak out narrow popular vote margins in states with a lot of Electoral College votes. He won Illinois' 22 electoral votes and Michigan's 13 electoral votes and Missouri's 16 electoral votes by winning the popular vote by slim margins.

New York's 36 electoral votes were the main determining factor. Harrison won New York's 36 Electoral College votes by getting 14,373 more popular votes than Cleveland (out of 1,319,748 votes cast). For the second presidential election in a row, a few voters in one state determined who would get to be president, and this time it *was not* the candidate who won the popular vote.

Unlike the election of 1824, there was little public outrage in the North over the fact that the candidate chosen by the people did not get to be president because it was common knowledge that hundreds of thousands of former slaves were being kept away from the polls in the

South. It was reasoned that those voters would have voted for Harrison if they had been given the opportunity.

Although there was little public outrage over the election of 1825, the result made it quite clear that close elections would continue to reveal the flaws of the Electoral College system.

The Presidential Election of 1892

The presidential election of 1892 demonstrated the same thing the election of 1824 had demonstrated: voters don't like it when the candidate they chose does not get to be president. They voted against the incumbent Benjamin Harrison and returned Grover Cleveland to the presidency.

Although the South was still solidly in the Democratic camp, six new northern states, Idaho, North Dakota, South Dakota, Montana, Washington, and Wyoming voted for the first time in a presidential election, and they mostly supported the Republicans. (In this 1892 election, Wyoming became the only state to allow women to vote.)

COMMENT:

Although Wyoming women were allowed to vote in the presidential election of 1892, **Women's suffrage** in the United States did not come easily.

There was no serious movement in the United States to allow women to vote until 1848 when Gerrit Smith, a candidate for president, made it part of his Liberty Party's platform. However, at that time, the idea didn't get much traction.

By the mid 1850s, there was still no concerted effort on the part of the all-male political establishment to allow women to vote. However, women were starting to get some legal rights. In some states, a woman could file for divorce, and a few states passed laws that said working women didn't have to turn over their wages to their husbands.

Some states, especially southern and rural states, were unwilling to give women *any* legal rights. A famous legal case in North Carolina made the point. A woman had appealed to change the state law so a woman would be allowed to file for divorce if she had been badly beaten by her husband. The state Supreme Court turned down her appeal in 1862, stating, "The law gives the husband power to use such a degree of force necessary to make the wife behave and know her place."

After the Civil War, there was some talk of Women's suffrage, but it took female activists like **Susan B. Anthony** to bring the issue to the public's attention. She and others like **Elizabeth Cady Stanton** organized women's rights gatherings and wrote books about the lack of women's legal rights in the U.S. Their books were intended to be read by women, but were also read by men. Some men voiced approval, but others tried to ban the books, saying for a women to have rights would be against the will of nature.

There was considerable resistance even among women's groups. Many women felt the suffragettes shouldn't be trying to change traditional women's roles.

Movements were formed to fight against the very idea of women gaining *any* legal rights, let alone the right to vote. One prominent organization was the **National Organization Against Women's Suffrage,** and it counted many women as members.

In 1869, Susan B. Anthony and Elizabeth Cady Stanton formed the **National Woman Suffrage Association (NWSA).** They lobbied for women's rights and proposed an amendment to the Constitution giving women the right to vote in all elections.

In 1890, several women's rights organizations came together to form the **National American Woman Suffrage Association** which was headed by **Carrie Chapman Catt.**

After Wyoming gave women the right to vote, lobbying efforts by Susan B. Anthony and others encouraged some of the other western states to follow suit, apparently in hopes of attracting more women to the still untamed and almost all male western territories.

Utah territory was one of the first western states to allow women the vote, but it was not activist women who were behind the effort; it was activist men who were trying to stamp out the practice of polygamy. A group of men known as **Godbeites** left the Latter Day Saints (Mormon) church and took up the fight against the church-condoned practice of men having multiple wives. They hoped women, if given the right to vote, would be freed from the male dominance officially sanctioned by the Mormon Church and would vote to end polygamy.

The practice of men having multiple wives was part of the Mormon religion, but the church's leader, Brigham Young, got behind the women's suffrage movement effort in hopes it would help change the image of Utah women as oppressed, and maybe even sidetrack anti-polygamy legislation that was working its way through Congress. With Brigham Young's support, there was no resistance to the idea, and in 1869, the territorial legislature passed an act giving women the vote (but not the right to run for office).

Paradoxically, the U.S. Congress overrode the new Utah act by passing the **Edmunds-Tucker Anti-polygamy Act**, which specifically banned voting by women in Utah. The movement to stamp out polygamy in Utah was gaining momentum across the nation, and it was becoming a major issue in every presidential election. There was even a call to send U.S. Army troops to Utah to put a stop to the practice.

In 1890, the Mormon Church leaders declared that the church would no longer sanction the practice of polygamy. With that controversy out of the way, Utah was granted statehood in 1896 and **the right of Utah women to vote was written into the new state's constitution**.

In1865, Republicans proposed the **Fourteenth Amendment** to the Constitution that would give the vote to the millions of newly-freed black **men**.

It was not until 1915, long after the Emancipation Proclamation had given all **men** the right to vote, that Congress passed the **Nineteenth Amendment** to the Constitution which prohibited the states from denying the right to vote based on sex. Even at that late date, with the country becoming more and more industrialized and all of the lower 48 states now part of the Union, only some western states and a few midwestern states had granted women the right to vote. **Until 1915, women were specifically barred from voting** even in local elections in all of the East Coast states and most of the southern states.

The Presidential Election of 1896

The presidential election of 1896 was contended mostly over economic matters. One contentious issue was about whether the U.S. should remain on **the gold standard**.

The Republicans nominated **William McKinley** who had served in the U.S. House of Representatives from Ohio, and as that state's governor.

The Democratic party was split over the issue of whether the U.S. should stay on the gold standard or not. After much contention, they nominated **William Jennings Bryan** who was against the gold standard and in favor of liberalizing the banking standards of the United States. Bryan was the youngest presidential nominee in American history, only one year older than the constitutional minimum of 35.

The election of 1896 was also one of the first elections in which campaign money played an important role. **The Republican campaign outspent the Democratic campaign by sixteen to one**.

With little money to mount an effective national advertising campaign, Bryan took to the railroads and went on a nationwide **whistle-stop campaign**. Up to that time, it was seen as unseemly for presidential candidates to actively go out and campaign for themselves, and the novelty of seeing a presidential candidate in person drew large crowds to Bryan's campaign stops. Outside of the large eastern cities, few had ever had the chance to listen to the powerful oratory of a skillful speaker.

In the end, money won out although the election was fairly close because the South again voted solidly for the Democrat as did a few of the western states. McKinley won by only about 600,000 votes out of almost 14 million votes cast.

The Presidential Election of 1900

The presidential election of 1900 turned out to be a rematch of the 1896 election. This time, McKinley chose New York's governor, **Theodore Roosevelt**, as his running mate. Although Roosevelt didn't want to give up his powerful position as the governor of the nation's most populous state just to be vice president, he finally relented. It was a decision that was to have significant ramifications for him and for the country.

Although Bryan again carried the South, this time, the election was not quite as close because McKinley managed to carry more of the western states.

In 1901, during a visit to the Pan-American Exposition in Buffalo, New York, McKinley was wounded in the stomach by an assassin's bullet. A local doctor could not find the bullet, and it was assumed the president had only been grazed. Although he suffered continuing digestive problems, he soon resumed his daily duties. What was not known to the doctors was that the bullet was still lodged in his stomach and gangrene was slowly killing the president. He died on September 14, 1901, and Roosevelt rushed to Washington to assume the duties of president.

The Presidential Election of 1904

The **presidential election of 1904** saw Republican **Theodore Roosevelt** running for his first full term as president against **Alton B. Parker**, a New York Supreme Court justice. Because Roosevelt had served a good part of the prior presidents term, he promised that if he was elected he would not to seek another term.

Parker, the Democrat, was relatively unknown, and he was going up against the popular and flamboyant Roosevelt. He was only able to carry the South, which, since Lincoln, continued to vote *against* the Republicans no matter who they put up. In fact, in Florida, Louisiana, Mississippi, and South Carolina, Roosevelt was only able to get a few thousand votes despite his overwhelming popularity everywhere else in the country.

The Presidential Election of 1908

Roosevelt was true to his promise not to seek another term, so for the presidential election of 1908, the Republicans put up **William H. Taft** who was Roosevelt's Secretary of War.

The Democrats, for the third time, put up **William Jennings Bryan**. Although Bryan was by then a very experienced presidential campaigner, his campaign was under funded. He was again only able to carry the South and a few of the western states.

Taft was elected by a comfortable margin.

The Presidential Election of 1912

The presidential election season in 1912 began with a potential European war in the background. As it turned out, it would mark the first presidential election since the ascendancy of the Republican and Democratic parties in which those two parties did not control essentially all of the Electoral College votes.

There were four serious candidates running for president in 1912. **Republican William H. Taft was** running for reelection. The **Democrats** ran **Woodrow Wilson**, the Governor of New Jersey and they chose **Thomas R. Marshall**, the governor of Indiana as his running mate. The **Socialist Party** ran **Eugene V. Debs. Theodore Roosevelt** decided to run for president again, but this time as the **Progressive Party's** candidate.

Although Roosevelt had promised not to run for reelection as president in 1908, he had a falling out with fellow Republican William Taft and decided to try to unseat him. He came in second in the voting, and in the end, all he accomplished was to help a Democrat get elected president for the first time since 1892.

Added together, Roosevelt and Taft received more votes than Wilson. However, they won only 96 Electoral College votes. Wilson received 453 Electoral College votes and was therefore elected the nation's 28th president.

Chapter Nine
The Politics of War

The Presidential Election of 1916

The **presidential election of 1916** took place against the backdrop of an ongoing bloody war in Europe. Wilson ran for reelection as a **Democrat** on a platform of keeping the U.S. out of the war. It was a popular position in 1916.

The **Republicans** put up Supreme Court Justice **Charles Evans Hughes**, who received the support of former president, Theodore Roosevelt.

The **Socialists** again put up a candidate, **A. L. Benson**, and although socialist ideas were gaining some popularity in the country, there was little chance he would win any Electoral College votes.

The popular vote was close with 9,126,868 votes going to Wilson and 8,548,728 votes going for Hughes. The Electoral College vote was also close, but Wilson was able to prevail 277 to 254. His 23 vote majority in the Electoral College meant it would have taken only one or two states to swing the Electoral College in the other direction. In many states outside of the South, the vote was very close.

COMMENT:

Despite the ongoing war in Europe, after the election of 1916, most Americans still wanted the United States to maintain its neutrality.

However, part of Germany's war effort was to use their fleet of U-boats (submarines) to attack and sink any ship that might be bringing supplies to England.

At that time, the United States was very dependent on its trade with England and other European countries that were allied with Britain. When the U.S. tried to maintain that trade despite the war, the German U-boats began to sink U.S. ships, and President Wilson began to threaten Germany with retaliation.

At about the same time, American officials learned Germany was trying to use the memory of the Mexican-American war to get Mexico to join Germany's war effort.

When that information was published by several U.S. newspapers, Americans were outraged. Although Wilson had promised in his campaign for the presidency to keep the United States out of the war in Europe, he now went before Congress to ask for a declaration of war against Germany.

Many Americans still wanted to stay out of the war, but throughout history, few members of Congress have dared to vote against going to war if a president requests it. On April 6, 1917, the Senate voted 82 to 6 to declare war on Germany. The House followed suit and voted 373 to 50 to allow the United States to enter **World War One** against the Germans.

The Presidential Election of 1920

Leading up to the **presidential election of 1920,** there was much turmoil in the country. In the early part of the twentieth century, labor unions were gaining considerable power, and they had begun using strikes as a tactic for improving wages and working conditions. Strife over labor issues led to race riots in several parts of the country. One race riot that pitted blacks and whites against each other in East St. Louis resulted in the deaths of more than one hundred African-Americans. Another riot erupted in Chicago when Irish groups fought African-Americans who were attempting to get jobs at the Chicago stockyards.

Because the previous several elections had been close, the two leading political parties tried to pick candidates from states with the most Electoral College votes. At that time, Ohio had 24 electoral votes, and as it turned out, both parties ended up picking candidates from that state.

The Democrats nominated Ohio Governor **James M. Cox**, and the Republicans chose Ohio Senator **Warren G. Harding**. Both had influence because both were newspaper publishers in an era when newspapers were becoming powerful political tools.

The Socialist again put up **Eugene V. Debs**, and although he was unable to win any Electoral College votes, he was able to capture almost a million popular votes.

The race between Harding and Cox did not turn out to be as close as everyone thought it would. Harding won Ohio easily, and he also won most of the other large states. Cox, the Democrat, carried all of the southern states, but it was not enough to win.

Warren G. Harding won the Electoral College vote and became the 29th president. In 1923, Harding died in office and his vice president, **Calvin Coolidge**, the former governor of Massachusetts, served out the last year of his term.

The Presidential Election of 1924

In the **presidential election of 1924,** Republican Coolidge, ran for reelection against Democrat **John W. Davis**, a prominent lawyer from West Virginia.

A third-party candidate, **Robert M. La Follette**, a **Progressive** from Wisconsin also ran. He was to become the most successful third-party candidate in the modern era. He won 4,831,706 votes and carried his home state of Wisconsin with its 13 Electoral College votes. However, this time, the election was not close enough for the presence of a third party candidate to throw the decision into the House of Representatives.

Although Davis, the Democrat, once again, carried the entire South, that was all he won. Coolidge was elected with a large majority in the Electoral College.

The Presidential Election of 1928

In the **presidential election of 1928,** Coolidge chose not to run for reelection, and the Republicans nominated **Herbert Hoover** from California, He had been the nation's Commerce Secretary under president Harding. At that point in time, it was one of the few times a candidate from the West had been nominated by a major party.

The Democrats nominated Governor **Al Smith** from New York, but unfortunately for him, many voters associated him with the well-publicized Tammany Hall corruption that had been going on in New York (even though he was not part of it). In addition, Smith was a Roman Catholic, and there was a widespread belief among Protestants that, if elected, he might take orders from the Pope.

Despite Smith's religion, he was still a Democrat going up against a Republican so he won all of the Protestant South except for Florida. After 68 years, the South was still voting *against* the Republicans, the party that had elected the hated Abraham Lincoln.

Hoover easily won the presidency by one of the largest pluralities in modern presidential election history.

COMMENT:

Religion has rarely played a role in presidential elections. Up until **Roman Catholic** Al Smith was the Democratic nominee for president in 1928, every candidate had been a Protestant. After Al Smith lost badly, neither the Democrats nor the Republicans nominated another Roman Catholic until Senator John Kennedy was nominated by the Democrats in 1960 (who won in a very close election despite much discussion about his religion).

Roman Catholic Senator John Kerry was nominated by the Democrats in 2004, and he lost in a close election. This time the focus was on the Vietnam war, and there was not much discussion about religion.

There has never been a Jewish candidate nominated for president by either the Democrats or the Republicans.

The Republican nomination of Mitt Romney for president in 2012 was the first time either party had nominated a Mormon for president. The question was, would his religion influence voters.

If we look back to the election of 1928, it tells us something important about voters and religion. In that election, the mostly Protestant South voted *for* the Democratic Roman Catholic nominee, Al Smith. The voters of the South of that era consistently voted *against* the Republicans, no matter what candidate they put forward. Today, that trend has reversed: now the South mostly votes for the Republican candidate. Although there was a lot of talk about Romney's Mormon religion, the conservative voters in the southern states, who had been consistently voting *against* whatever candidate the Democrats nominated, continued to do so. The south voted for Mitt Romney, regardless of the religion he practiced.

The Presidential Election of 1932

The **presidential election of 1932** took place in the middle of the Great Depression.

The Democrats nominated **Franklin D. Roosevelt**, the wealthy governor of New York. He chose John Nance Garner IV from Texas as his running mate.

The Republicans put up **Hoover** for reelection, but with the economy being in such bad shape, few gave him much of a chance to hold onto the presidency.

During the campaign, there was some talk about Roosevelt's health being an issue. Roosevelt had contracted polio in 1921 and the infection left him permanently paralyzed from the waist down. At that time, polio (poliomyelitis) was a common childhood disease and outbreaks of the disease were all too common during the summer months, especially in large cities. There was no cure at that time and there still isn't; however, a vaccine was developed, and due to a nearly universal vaccination program, the disease is rare today.

Roosevelt learned to get around a bit with the help of leg braces and canes, and at home he used a wheelchair. However, for the rest of his life, he was careful to never be seen by the public in that wheelchair. The most famous pictures of him, such as in the back seat of his convertible, or on the deck of the USS Quincy at the end of WWII, always showed him sitting down.

The election was a landslide for Roosevelt. Hoover only won six Northeastern states, Connecticut, Delaware, Maine, New Hampshire, Pennsylvania, and Vermont, and even in those states his margin of victory was very slim.

The Presidential Election of 1936

With the depression still going on, **Roosevelt** ran for reelection in **1936**. His running mate was again John Garner.

The Republicans nominated **Alf Landon**, the governor of Kansas.

For the Democrats, there was some concern that Roosevelt might lose the South, and other conservative states because the Republicans were aggressively attacking him as a socialist. They claimed his "**New Deal**" policies, including Social Security and unemployment relief, were taking the United States down the road toward socialism.

But Roosevelt needn't have worried because, once again, he carried every southern state. In fact, in the southern states where African-Americans were systematically kept from voting, the Republican candidate hardly got any votes at all. For example, in Mississippi, Landon got only 4,443 votes, and in South Carolina he only got 1,646 votes. It was clear that even 76 years after Lincoln's election, the conservative South was still voting *against* Lincoln and the Republicans, even if it meant voting for a very liberal (and some said *socialist*) candidate.

Roosevelt surprised everyone (including some pollsters) by carrying every state except Maine and Vermont. His Electoral College win was 523 to 8.

COMMENT:

The Great Depression, like all economic downturns, influenced presidential elections and presidential policy for many years. It was the main reason Hoover was overwhelmingly rejected by the voters, and it was the main reason Roosevelt was able to enact many of his new programs (most of Roosevelt's New Deal programs were attacked by the Republicans, and later some of the programs were declared unconstitutional).

Although there were some fundamental problems in the U.S. economy before 1929, the depression is usually thought to have begun on "**Black Tuesday**," October 29, 1929. That day the U.S. stock market dropped dramatically. The downturn had actually begun the week before when a smaller downturn scared some investors, and the following Monday many of them chose to get out of the market. The next day, Black Tuesday, even more investors sold out and a huge number of shares were traded. Stocks fell an average of twelve percent.

William C. Durant and **the Rockefeller family** saw the fall in stock prices as an opportunity to buy them at historically low prices, so they stepped in and bought stocks in large quantities. That helped convince some investors that the market was safe, but after a bit of recovery, the market began to fall again.

Investors like **John D. Rockefeller** tried to talk about a stock market comeback, but many ordinary citizens had begun to invest in the market, and they had lost money in the downturn. In order to attract investors, stock brokers were in the habit of lending small investors money to buy stocks, so it was not just stock speculators that were wiped out. Many people reacted to the decreasing stock values by taking their money out of the stock market, *and* they began to spend less to make up for their losses. That started a cycle of business slowdown and job layoffs, which led to even less spending.

It didn't help that the midwestern plains states were suffering from an extended drought that eventually led to what was referred to as the "**dust bowl**" (the drying out and blowing away of rich agricultural soil).

President Hoover's response to the economic slowdown was to try to pressure businesses to keep workers employed and to keep wages high. That didn't work very well because the businesses were under too much pressure from decreasing sales. Hoover did lower some taxes, but at first he was opposed to the government getting involved in job programs or putting money into the economy in any other way. Instead, he believed churches and private charities should take up the challenge. As for government back-to-work programs, he said that was up to local and state governments.

When the depression worsened, Hoover *did* begin to institute some large-scale government job-creation programs. The huge Hoover Dam project on the Colorado River is one example.

As the 1932 election approached, many U.S. citizens blamed the economic downturn on Hoover, and whether or not that was a fair judgment, it led to his loss to Franklin Roosevelt.

The Presidential Election of 1940

By the time the presidential election of 1940 came around, the economy was improving and all attention was on the war in Europe. The country was divided as to whether the U.S. should go to the aid of England and France.

John Garner, Roosevelt's vice president, assumed Roosevelt would stick to tradition and not run for a third term, so he decided to make a run for the presidency on the Democratic ticket. He was much more conservative than Roosevelt and disagreed with much of the New Deal agenda. As a result, he had much wider support in the South and in the conservative rural states. However, Democratic President Roosevelt soon decided to break with tradition and run for a third term. He chose his Secretary of Commerce, **Henry Wallace** from Iowa.

After the Republicans were unable to agree on a candidate, a surprising dark horse named **Wendell Willkie** came forward. He was an industrialist from Indiana who had never been much involved in politics.

Throughout the election, the Republicans focused on Roosevelt's perceived failure to end the depression and his apparent willingness to get the United States involved in the ongoing war in Europe. Roosevelt responded by saying it was his New Deal programs that were ending the Great Depression, and he said he had no intention of getting involved in the European war.

Again, there was talk that Roosevelt was too liberal, and that meant he would lose the conservative South.

In 1940, it did seem possible that a Republican could win the South because a "conservative coalition" had emerged in Congress that brought together conservative southern Democrats with conservative Republicans. By election time, they had already been successful at defeating *some* of Roosevelt's liberal New Deal policies. Many thought the two groups would work together to defeat Roosevelt in the upcoming presidential election. However, it didn't work out that way. The citizens of the South continued to vote straight Democratic. They were still unwilling to vote for the hated "Lincoln-Republicans," no matter how liberal Roosevelt was.

The East also went for Roosevelt, except once again, conservative Maine and Vermont voted against him.

COMMENT:

When Franklin D. Roosevelt ran for an unprecedented third term, and again when he ran for a fourth term, the Republicans pointed out the fact that George Washington had declined to run for a third term as president. They said President Washington's decision indicated the founding fathers had wanted to limit the time a president could serve.

Based on that reasoning, they introduced a measure to amend the Constitution to limit the number of terms a person could hold the presidency. It was passed and the result was the Twenty-Second Amendment which limited any one individual's term of presidency to two terms. It was ratified by three-fourths of the states on February 27, 1951.

The Presidential Election of 1944

By the time the presidential election of 1944 came around, the nation was at war. Germany's ally, **the Japanese, had attacked the U.S. naval base at Pearl Harbor in Hawaii** and it immediately drew the United States into **World War Two**.

As the fall election approached, the entire country was focused on winning what was turning out to be a very difficult war.

Every family had somebody involved "over there" and casualties were high. Most of the families in America dreaded the arrival of the telegraph man, sure that any news from Europe would be bad news.

In addition, nearly every family in the country was either working on something related to the war effort, or suffering restrictions because of it. Although the war was taking place far away, there was a feeling that if the Germans and the Japanese were not stopped "over there," they would soon arrive on our shores. As a result, the people were probably less involved in the election of 1944 than any previous election.

For the 1944 presidential election, the **Republicans** put up **Thomas E. Dewey**, the governor of New York. He chose **John Bricker**, the Governor of Ohio, as his running mate.

It was no surprise when **Roosevelt ran for reelection in 1944**, this time with Harry S. Truman as his vice president. With the U.S. in the middle of a war, most thought Roosevel would be reelected.

Dewey campaigned hard against Roosevelt, saying four terms for a president was too many. Some accused the president of trying to become a king. Others continued to **try to paint him as a socialist**, pointing out that some of his New Deal programs had been declared unconstitutional, and others had been overturned in Congress (mostly through the efforts of the conservative coalition).

By the time the election campaign was underway, the economy was improving, helping Roosevelt's chances. In addition, U.S. troops had landed on the beaches of Normandy on June 6, 1944, and although American casualties were heavy, the invasion was a success. Within days, U.S. troops were pushing inland in France.
By the end of August, U.S. troops were in Paris, and there had been a string of successful battles against Japan in the Pacific. By election day, U.S. troops were at the Germany border.

The military successes of that summer were enough to convince most U.S. citizens that Roosevelt was running the war properly .

Roosevelt was reelected for a fourth term, again winning all of the southern states. However, much of the conservative Midwest voted against Roosevelt, and Dewey, the Republican candidate, actually got quite a few votes in some of the southern states. The conservative versus liberal message was beginning to gain some traction in the South. For example, although Roosevelt won North Carolina, Dewey managed to get 263,155 votes. In West Virginia, where Roosevelt had won easily in 1940, Dewey got 322,819 votes.

However, in the deep South, the people had still not forgiven the Republicans for electing Lincoln. They still voted for the Democrat, no matter who he was. And although Roosevelt had nearly unanimous support among the large African-American population in the South, there were still restriction in place to try to keep them from voting.

The people of the South that were allowed to vote voted for the liberal Democrat Roosevelt in overwhelm numbers. For example, in Mississippi, Dewey only got 11,601 votes.

Nationwide, the popular vote was fairly close, 25,612,916 for Roosevelt and 22,017,929 for Dewey. But the Electoral College vote was not close. It came out 432 for Roosevelt and only 99 for Dewey.

Roosevelt died after only a few months into his fourth term. His vice president, **Harry Truman,** was sworn in as president, and he presided over the last few months of the war, including the atomic bomb attacks on Japan.

COMMENT:

World War Two did not play as much of a role in U.S. presidential politics as you might think. Although the war did influence the voting that took place prior to the election of 1940 when Wendell Willkie accused Roosevelt of trying to get the U.S involved in what they saw as a European war, Roosevelt's promise to keep the country out of the war defused Willkie's attack.

But when Japan attacked the American naval base at Pearl Harbor, nearly all Americans supported Roosevelt when he went on the radio to tell the country he had asked Congress for a declaration of war on Japan. **His "day of infamy" speech** was a rallying cry for the U.S. to enter the war on the side of the allies. He issued a presidential order that said any government agency that was in any way related to the war effort would report directly him. He ordered many corporations to modify their manufacturing lines to make war materials and established a goal of producing 10,000 new fighter airplanes per year. He also ordered an emergency shipbuilding program to quickly build ships to carry troops and war material.

The **Selective Service Act** was passed with Roosevelt's help, and when the U.S. declared war on Japan and Germany, all men in the United States between the ages of 16 to 65 were required to register for the draft.

Millions of young men were drafted into the Army and millions more voluntarily signed up to serve in one of the military branches.

It is a little known fact that the Selective Service Act even provided a role for those who were, for reasons of religion or personal belief, unwilling to fight in wars. It said they would not be required to undergo combat training but would instead undergo training for noncombatant support roles.

America's isolationist stance had left the country unprepared to fight a war, but once war was declared, most citizens were willing to make sacrifices to help. In 1944, most people felt that included supporting and voting for President Roosevelt.

The Presidential Election of 1948

In 1948, Truman ran for reelection. He was nominated by the Democrats, and he chose U.S. Senator **Alben Barkley** as his running mate.

The Republicans again nominated **Thomas Dewey** and his running mate, Earl Warren, the Governor of California.

Henry A. Wallace, Roosevelt's former vice president, was also on the ballot as a **Progressive Party** candidate.

Despite the national joy that the war was finally over, Truman was not popular. There was trouble brewing in Asia and elsewhere as an aftermath of the war, and there was some unease about the fact that Truman had ordered atomic bombs dropped on innocent Japanese civilians when many thought the war was all but over anyhow. There was also concern about what was going on in Europe. The division of Berlin between the Eastern and Western powers was still unsettled, and Russia's blockade of Berlin was an indication of the cold war that would develop between Russia and the United States.

There was also the first signs that the South was no longer going to just blindly vote for Democrats.

At the Democratic national nominating convention, Truman had promised to introduce **civil rights legislation**. Hearing that, the southern Democratic delegates all got up and walked out. They held their own convention in Birmingham, Alabama and nominated Senator Strom Thurmond from South Carolina as a **States' Right Democrat**.

Thurmond ran on a segregationist platform and managed to squeak out wins in Alabama and Louisiana. He won his home state of South Carolina and he won Mississippi overwhelmingly.

The first results showed the election was very close. Truman had lost *some* of the South, *some* of the Midwest, but he won the Northeast and the West coast.

Some newspapers came out the morning after the election with mistaken banner headlines declaring "**Dewey Wins**," but when the long process of counting of ballots was finally finished, Truman had won after all with 24,179,347 nationwide popular votes over Dewey's 21,991,292 votes.

The final Electoral College vote was Truman 303, Dewey 189, and Thurmond 39.

Thurmond's wins in the South marked the first time in the modern era that a third-party candidate had won a significant number of electoral votes. Had the election in the northern states been closer, it would have thrown the decision about who would be president into the House of Representatives.

Chapter Ten
Postwar and Cold War Politics

The Presidential Election of 1952

In **1952**, the Republicans finally managed to convince **World War Two hero**, General **Dwight D. Eisenhower**, to run for president. They had tried to convince him to run in 1948, but he had refused. This time they told him it was his duty to the country, and he finally accepted. Because the **Cold War** with Russia was bound to be one of the main election issues, he chose noted anti-Communist, **Richard Nixon** from California, as his running mate.

The Democrats were in a quandary because Truman, the incumbent, had decided not to run. By 1952, primary elections to select a party's candidate were becoming the norm and in the Democratic primaries, Governor **Adlai Stevenson II** of Illinois was showing well. He was nominated at the 1952 Democratic national presidential nominating convention in Chicago. In an attempt to recapture the southern vote, he selected **John Jackson Sparkman from Alabama** as his running mate.

There was little doubt about the popularity of General Eisenhower, but some of his opinions were very controversial. He was a strong believer in the United Nations, and thought that organization could better control the expansion of nuclear weapons than the United States could. Those kinds of non-nationalistic opinions were strongly opposed by **Republican Senator Joseph McCarthy** who was beating the drums of nationalism and stirring up anti-Communist "witch hunts" through the use of his congressional committee that was finding anti-American Communist spies under every rock. He said there were "commies" everywhere, including, he said, within the entertainment industry and even deep inside the U.S. government.

Two years before, the **Korean War** had flared up as a result of the postwar division of that country. The conflict was showing signs of expanding into a showdown with China, and maybe even Russia. This time the people of the United States were not so enthusiastic about getting involved in another war because they were still recovering from the depravation and losses in Second World War.

By 1952, Russia had developed its own atomic bomb, and Joseph Stalin, the Russian Premier was making threatening comments toward the U.S. In the face of such threats, what the United States needed was a hero. Eisenhower, the famous General, fit that bill. He was elected by a large majority in the Electoral College, 442 to 89, to be the first Republican in the White House in 20 years.

As usual, the South mostly went to the Democrats. Stevenson won most of the southern states by large majorities. However, for the first time in many years, a few southern states, Florida, Tennessee, and Virginia, went for the Republican candidate, although by narrow majorities in each case. After 92 years, cracks in the anti-Lincoln, anti-Republican southern attitude were beginning to show.

COMMENT:

The **Korean War** was one of the Asian conflicts that flared up after World War Two over who would control a country after the Japanese were forced to withdraw.

Without consulting the Koreans, the allies decided to divide the country north and south. In 1950, armed conflict broke out between the divided sections.

As the conflict escalated, the North Koreans were supported by the People's Republic of China and Russia (the Union of Soviet Socialist Republics), while the South Koreans were being supported by the United States. It was to become the first armed conflict of the so-called "**cold war**" that pitted the U.S. against what was seen as a Communist agenda to control the post-war world. From the U.S. point of view, the "war" was mostly against Russia, but there was also talk about a threat from Communist China.

With the support of the U.S. military, the South Koreans invaded the North, only to be pushed back when the Chinese army came to the aid of the North Koreans.

In 1953, an uneasy stalemate was reached along the 38th parallel that divided the country north and south. A **Demilitarized Zone** along that line still maintains the stalemate to this day. Democratic South Korea has developed a thriving economy based on manufacturing and export, while North Korea has retreated into a secretive Communist dictatorship which has, reportedly, pushed most of its citizens into poverty. Nevertheless, many South Koreans still hope for eventual unification.

The Presidential Election of 1956

In 1956, **Eisenhower** again ran against **Adlai Stevenson**.

The cold war was still going on, but Senator McCarthy had been discredited leaving most Americans less worried about communist infiltration here at home. Nevertheless, despite the country being in a period of peace and prosperity, the U.S. military was actively pursuing development of every more powerful nuclear weapons in response to a perceived threat from Russia that was doing the same.

With the Korean War becoming only a memory, and the U.S. economy doing well, Eisenhower was assured another term. He won every state outside of the South, and even there he picked up a few more states than in the previous election, squeaking out wins in Kentucky and West Virginia. However, Eisenhower was soundly beaten by Stevenson in the traditionally anti-Republican states of Mississippi and South Carolina.

Despite the strength of the Democratic Party in the South, voters were beginning to rebel. The South had a long history of voting *against* the Republican candidate no matter who he was, but many southern voters were starting to resist voting for Democratic candidates they saw as northern liberals who were threatening to pass new legislation to break down the southern policy of strict segregation and give African-Americans more civil rights. In the 1956 election, some southern Democratic leaders broke with the national Democratic Party and tried to manipulate the Electoral College outcome by getting a slate of "**unpledged**" electors onto the ballot. (An unpledged elector has not pledged to support any particular candidate for President.) With unpledged electors on the ballot, voters could register their displeasure with the Democratic Party's candidate, in this case, Adlai Stevenson.

In Alabama, the unpledged electors got 20,150 votes. In Louisiana, they got 44,520 votes. In Mississippi, they got 42,266 votes (seventeen percent of the total vote), and in South Carolina, they got 88,509 votes (almost thirty percent of the total vote). In fact, in South Carolina, although Stevenson won, the unpledged electors got more votes than Eisenhower. It was clear voting patterns were changing in the South. Although the unpledged electors were unable to win any states, it was a sign of things to come in the South.

For the first time, political television advertising played a significant role in a presidential election, with much of the TV advertising aimed at women voters.

The Presidential Election of 1960

In 1960, Eisenhower's vice president, Californian **Richard Nixon**, was nominated by the Republicans to run against the Democratic nominee, **John F. Kennedy,** the young senator from Massachusetts.

From the beginning, everyone knew it was going to be a close election. The economy was not doing all that well, and the Russian launch of the world's first satellite, Sputnik, gave Americans the feeling that the U.S. was falling behind.

There was even talk that the election would end up in the House of Representatives because there was a movement underway in the South to take votes away from Kennedy who was seen as too liberal and very likely to introduce legislation that would outlaw segregation and end discrimination against African-Americans.

Nixon, despite having served as vice president under the fairly liberal Eisenhower, was known as a conservative. Many thought he would be a more appealing candidate for southern voters. People speculated that the Democratic Party's hold on the South was about to end, which would dramatically change future American presidential elections.

The **1960 election introduced televised debates** leading many to speculate that the election would be won or lost by how well the candidates came across on the small screen. Analysis of the four televised debates revealed an odd fact: those who heard the debates on the radio thought Nixon did very well, but those who watched the debates on television thought he did very poorly against the calm and polished Kennedy. It was becoming clear that television was going to be the way people learned about the candidates.

By the election of 1960, Alaska and Hawaii had been admitted to the Union and the citizens of the two newest states would finally be able to participate in a presidential election. However, with only six electoral votes between them, they didn't get much attention from the candidates.

The real election battleground was in the South. To help him win the southern States, Kennedy chose **Texan Lyndon B. Johnson** as his running mate.

Despite much negative talk about Kennedy being a Catholic, he held onto the predominantly Protestant southern states of Georgia, Louisiana, North Carolina, and South Carolina. But the emerging conservative movement in the South cost him Florida, Kentucky, Tennessee, and Virginia.

The conservatives managed to elect a slate of unpledged electors in Mississippi. In fact, in that state, the unpledged electors received more votes than either Nixon or Kennedy. Therefore, they won all eight of that state's electoral votes. In Alabama, Nixon received more votes than Kennedy, but the majority of the state's voters voted for the six unpledged conservative electors who, it was clear, were not going to cast their Electoral College votes for either Kennedy or Nixon.

When the Electoral College met to cast their ballots, all of the unpledged electors cast their votes for segregationists Harry F. Byrd and Strom Thurmond.

Nevertheless, Kennedy managed to win enough Electoral College votes to be elected president. The final Electoral College vote was Kennedy 303, Nixon 219, and Harry Byrd 15.

COMMENT:

As in most close elections, there were accusations of voter fraud in favor of Kennedy, especially in Mayor Daley's Chicago, and in Johnson's home state of Texas. Investigators later found that in some counties in Texas, more votes were cast for the Kennedy-Johnson ticket than there were voters in that county.

As soon as Kennedy was elected, he instituted new domestic programs and set about to change the nation's foreign policy. At home, he reinvigorated the space program and promised a balanced budget.

The Republicans, said Kennedy was soft on communism, but in the spring of 1961, he authorized a plan to try to overthrow the Communist government of Cuba. The CIA and the U.S. military landed 1500 former Cubans near the **Bay of Pigs** on the remote south side of the island of Cuba. They had been trained by the U.S. military in guerrilla tactics and were supposed to rally the people against Fidel Castro's government. However, the Cuban military soon killed or rounded up all of the guerrillas, and the U.S. was forced to pay a ransom to get the survivors back.

Then, in October of 1962, CIA U-2 spy planes photographed missile sites being built by Russian technicians in Cuba. It was possible the missiles could be used in a future nuclear attack on the United States.
It was the greatest crisis of Kennedy's administration. The military wanted to immediately bomb the missile sites, but Kennedy was afraid that would lead to a direct confrontation with Russia, with the potential that it could escalate into nuclear war. Kennedy decided on a naval blockade of Cuba until the missiles were removed.

Tension with Russia mounted until a deal was secretly struck. Russia's Premier, Nikita Khrushchev, agreed to dismantle the missile sites in Cuba if the U.S. would dismantle its missile sites in Turkey and promise never to invade Cuba. Kennedy agreed.

The "**Cuban Missile Crisis**" as it came to be known, quieted Republican criticism of Kennedy as being soft on communism and considerably enhanced Kennedy's approval rating.

In November of 1963, President Kennedy was on a visit to Dallas. He was riding in the back seat of a convertible limousine when he was shot and killed by Lee Harvey Oswald, a former Marine marksman who had positioned himself above the street in a 6th floor window of a nearby building.

Lyndon Johnson was immediately sworn in as president to serve out the last year of the presidency before the election of 1964.

Chapter Eleven
The Politics of War and Antiwar

The Presidential Election of 1964

In 1964, sitting president **Lyndon Johnson** was nominated for reelection by the **Democrats**. Johnson's only serious competition in those primaries came from **Alabama's governor George Wallace** who had come to national prominence when he stood in the doorway of the University of Alabama to block the entrance of black students. The event was covered on live TV.

Wallace's name appeared on three of the sixteen states that were holding Democratic presidential primaries that year, Wisconsin, Indiana, and Maryland. Running on a segregationist platform, Wallace won a surprising number of votes in those states.

COMMENT:

George Wallace's infamous "**stand in the schoolhouse door**" came about after the United States Supreme Court handed down a decision that state taxpayer-supported universities could not legally refuse to admit students because of their race. Most states complied to one degree or another, but the University of Alabama, with the support of the state's governor and other leading politicians, found ways to reject a student application if they found out the student had *any* African-American heritage.

When the University of Alabama refused to accept the applications of three fully-qualified African-American students, the students went to court. A federal judge ordered them to be admitted.

When the three student arrived on the opening day of classes, Governor Wallace was there in the doorway with local police to block their entrance. He had made sure there would be plenty of news media present to record the confrontation, and the national TV networks carried the event live for all the nation to watch.

Knowing ahead of time what was going to happen, President Kennedy federalized the Alabama National Guard and ordered them to make sure the students were admitted, by force if necessary.

The students were admitted, but it gained Wallace a big following throughout the South and that emboldened him to make a run for the presidency of the United States.

Despite Wallace's presence in the race, at the Democratic national nominating convention, Johnson won easily. He chose U.S. Senator **Hubert Humphrey** from Minnesota as his running mate.

The Republicans nominated **Barry Goldwater**, a conservative from Arizona. He chose Congressman **William E. Miller** from New York as his running mate.

Continuing the trend started in 1960, the candidates primarily used television to get their message across to the public. In the presidential election of 1964, television "attack" ads began to evolve into the unrelenting barrage of attack ads we see in today's political campaigns.

Johnson's ads used skillfully done movie-like scenarios to portray what might happen if Goldwater was elected. The infamous "**Daisy Girl**" **ad** showed an innocent-looking little girl picking petals from a daisy in a field of flowers. As she counted the flower's petals, the screen morphed into a missile launch countdown followed by a dramatic nuclear explosion. The ads were in response to Goldwater's statement that nuclear weapons might have to be used in some circumstances. Although it didn't come right out and accuse Goldwater of being an advocate of nuclear war, the ad effectively made the point that Goldwater's opinions could lead the country in that dangerous direction.

By 1964, the conservative wing of the Republicans was gaining control of the party. They turned away from Nixon because he was seen as too liberal, and instead chose conservative Senator **Barry Goldwater.** Governor Nelson Rockefeller of New York made a bid for the Republican nomination, but he too was seen as politically too moderate.

The 1964 presidential election gave the people a clear choice. They could vote for the outspokenly conservative and anti-Communist Goldwater, or the avowed liberal Johnson who wanted to create a "great society" through government policy.

Through television advertising, Johnson was able to paint Goldwater as a dangerous anti-Communist radical who might get the U.S. into a direct conflict with the Russians.

Paradoxically, Johnson was already secretly getting the country more deeply involved in the cold war against the Communists. As the election campaign progressed, U.S. forces were beginning to engage enemy forces in Vietnam. President Johnson was fully aware of the worsening situation there, but he didn't want the war to be at the forefront of the American public's attention with the election coming up.

Johnson won most of the nation in a landslide, but Goldwater carried Alabama, Georgia, Louisiana, Mississippi, and South Carolina. It was the first time a Republican had carried that much of the deep South, and it marked the end of a one hundred year dominance of Democrats in the region. That change in voting preferences was to have a profound effect on every presidential election from then on.

COMMENT:

By the time Johnson won the election in the fall of 1964, **U.S. forces were secretly becoming more engaged in combat in Vietnam.**

Years before, President Eisenhower had told President Kennedy that he believed the U.S. would end up having to send troops to Vietnam. After soviet Premier Nikita Khrushchev said Russia would support the North Vietnamese Communists, Eisenhower predicted Vietnam would be the next hot spot in the escalating "cold war."

In 1961, Johnson, as vice president, had visited President Diem in South Vietnam and hailed him as the "Winston Churchill of Asia."

Soon after that visit, skirmishes with troops from North Vietnam began. In response, President Kennedy sent a few hundred Green Beret "advisors" to South Vietnam to help train the South Vietnamese Army.

When more attacks on South Vietnam came from the north, Vietnamese President Diem requested more military aid from Kennedy. In response, Kennedy sent General Maxwell Taylor to Vietnam to access the situation. Taylor came back alarmed at what he had seen and told Kennedy that if Vietnam fell into the hands of the Communists, all of Southeast Asia would eventually fall.

The Pentagon advised Kennedy's Defense Secretary Robert McNamara that a massive show of force was needed. McNamara concurred and suggested to Kennedy that the U.S. should send at least 20,000 troops to Vietnam. Kennedy decided against it, and to this day there is discussion about whether the U.S. would have gotten so deeply involved in Vietnam had Kennedy not been assassinated.

Kennedy *did* continue to send advisors to Vietnam (eventually more than 16,000), and he also sent helicopter units. In the fall of 1961, he guaranteed President Diem that the United States would help Vietnam "preserve its independence."

In 1962, a reporter asked President Kennedy if any Americans in Vietnam were engaged in the fighting there. The president said no, but in fact, they were. U.S. pilots were participating in bombing runs using U.S. aircraft. Some of the bomb attacks were resulting in civilian causalities, and after seeing American planes doing the bombing, many South Vietnamese blamed the Americans.

Defense Secretary McNamara visited South Vietnam during the summer of 1962 and came back to tell President Kennedy that the South Vietnamese war against the northern invaders was going well because of U.S. help.

Soon after that visit, the first U.S. Special Forces base was secretly established at Khe Sanh.

When Buddhists rioters in South Vietnam took to the streets in Saigon to protest a government crackdown on religion, they were fired on by South Vietnamese troops. Several Buddhist monks publicly burned themselves to death as an act of protest.

The worldwide publicity from those acts brought Vietnam to the attention of American citizens for the first time. Some citizen groups began asking what we were doing over there, and reports began to circulate that the U.S. was supporting a corrupt government in Vietnam.

Soon, a coup was mounted against President Diem, resulting in the assassination of Diem and his brother. Later evidence showed that the CIA had at least tacitly supported the coup.

By the time Kennedy was assassinated in November 24, 1963, the situation in Vietnam was becoming very unstable. Viet Cong guerrillas were occupying more and more of the countryside.

As soon as President Johnson was sworn in, he took over management of the war. At press conferences, he began making strong statements that the U.S. would not allow the Communists to take Vietnam.

At first, President Johnson made sure most of the U.S. involvement in the Vietnam War was being done covertly. Secret U.S. bombing raids, using U.S. airplanes and "volunteer" American pilots, were attacking Viet Cong bases both in Vietnam and in Laos.

Defense Secretary McNamara began making more and more public statements indicating that the U.S. would support the new Vietnamese military government. He said, "We'll stay for as long as it takes."

After that, America was committed. Johnson believed the reputation of the U.S. (and his personal reputation) was on the line.

But when word leaked out that our "support" of the South Vietnamese was already costing the U.S. more than two million dollars a day, more people began to ask if it was such a good idea to be committing those kinds of resources in a tiny and relatively unknown country half way around the world.

Johnson continued to try to keep the war low profile, mainly because he knew he didn't have the support in Congress for another Asian war so soon after the debacle in Korea.

He mostly used the CIA to conduct secret operations out of Saigon, and he used U.S. Navy warships to harass North Vietnamese installations along the coast.

Meanwhile, in Vietnam, the increasing successes of the Viet Cong were causing political instability. In one year, South Vietnam saw five different governments come into power.

In the summer of 1964, President Johnson was preoccupied with running for election. He named Lt. Gen William C. Westmoreland to oversee operations in Vietnam.

Senator Barry Goldwater, Johnson's very conservative Republican opponent in the election, was trying to use the lack of more aggressive action in Vietnam to paint Johnson as soft on communism.

At the beginning of August, only a few months before the presidential election was to take place, the "**Gulf of Tonkin Incident**" took place. It involved U.S. war ships that were supporting South Vietnamese speed boats that were staging attacks on North Vietnamese coastal installations. North Vietnamese torpedo boats came out to respond and were shelled by the USS Maddox, a Sumner-class destroyer. It was reported that at least one of the torpedo boats fired back, and that one 14.5 mm round hit the destroyer. The round didn't cause any serious damage on the Maddox, and no one was injured. Later that same day, a second attack was reported.

As minor as the incident had been, it was nevertheless the excuse Johnson had been looking for to show he was not soft on communism. He went on the radio to describe two attacks by North Vietnamese vessels against U.S. Navy ships "on the high seas." In his speech, he did not indicate that the U.S. was already involved in Vietnam in any way other than in a supporting role. The implication of his speech was that the North Vietnamese had launched an unprovoked attack on a U.S. ship that was just minding its own business out in international waters.

The truth, as we later learned, was that **neither Johnson nor McNamara were sure there really had been an attack**, and later the captain of one of the ships involved said the second attack might have actually been a false radar image.

There was some resistance in Congress to getting involved in yet another Asian war, but after some deliberation they passed the **Tonkin Gulf Resolution** which authorized President Johnson to use "conventional" military force in Southeast Asia. Significantly, it was not a formal declaration of war by Congress. Although it is now usually referred to as "The Vietnam War," it was actually termed a "**police action**," or simply, a "**conflict.**" Looking back, "police action" is an odd euphemism for a conflict that involved all branches of the U.S. military and that is estimated to have **cost the lives of 58,272 American soldiers, 266,000 Army of the Republic of Vietnam soldiers, 1,100,000 North Vietnamese Army and Viet Cong soldiers, and an estimated 843,000 Vietnamese civilians**. In addition, **303,644 American soldiers were wounded in action**, not counting those that suffered from **post-traumatic stress disorder (PTSD)** as a result of what they experienced in Vietnam.

As the war was escalated, there were a few protests against it back home in the U.S. However, as the news media began sending back horrific reports about what was going on over there, often showing footage of the actual fighting on the nightly TV news, the protests increased. Eventually, some of the antiwar protests attracted as many as half a million people.

The **Viet Cong's Tet offensive** in January of 1968 further undermined U.S. support for the war. Popular CBS anchorman Walter Cronkite went on TV to say that in his opinion the U.S. was mired in an unwinnable stalemate in Vietnam.

On March 31, 1968, President Johnson went on live television to announce that he would not seek reelection, saying, "There is division in the American house now."

His 1964 campaign promise of creating a "great society" had been ruined when his focus turned to combating communism, causing him to escalate a pointless war in Vietnam that ended in complete failure. By the end of his presidency, there was no great society, only a divided nation that was deeply involved in a war that was costing the country untold amounts of money and many thousands of American lives.

The Presidential Election of 1968

In 1968, Johnson's decision not to run for reelection meant the 1968 race for the presidency would be wide open. Everyone knew the election would be a referendum on the Vietnam War.

Richard Nixon, Eisenhower's former vice president threw his hat into the ring. His two main Republican rivals were Michigan Governor George W. Romney (Mitt Romney's father) and California Governor Ronald Reagan.

There were clear choices between the Republican candidates. Nixon and Reagan were both saying America had to be tough on communism, and Vietnam was a key test of America's resolve.

Romney had voted for the **Tonkin Gulf Resolution,** and he had been an early supporter of the war. But now he said Vietnam was a mistake. He said he had been "brainwashed" by the military into supporting the Vietnam War. That remark cost him votes in the Republican primaries.

Both Nixon and Reagan knew the Democrats were likely to run somebody who would make ending the Vietnam War a priority. In order to make the election about fighting communism, Nixon and Reagan tried to show they would be tougher on communism, and that they would win the war in Vietnam. Much of Nixon's oratory was to rail against the anti-war protesters that he characterized as un-American supporters of worldwide communism.

By the end of the Republican primaries, it was clear Republican voters were responding to Nixon's pro-war, anti-Communist message. There were a few antiwar protests at the **Republican national presidential nominating convention**, but most of the Republicans in attendance were in favor of continuing what they saw as a fight against Communist aggression.

Nixon was nominated and as part of the new Republican "**southern strategy**," he selected Maryland Governor Spiro Agnew as his running mate.

The **Democratic national presidential nominating convention** was anything but peaceful. Held in Chicago, it attracted many thousands of antiwar protesters who gathered outside the convention center. Mayor Richard Daley brought in 23,000 police and National Guardsmen to control the situation, and many of the protesters were beaten and arrested. Unfortunately for the Democrats, all this was shown on live TV, disrupting the coverage of the convention and making the Democrats, or at least the Chicago police, seem unnecessarily cruel. The **Walker Report**, a federal investigation of what happened, characterized it as "a police riot." The report blamed Mayor Richard J. Daley for what it called "unrestrained and indiscriminate police violence."

The assassinations of the leading Democratic presidential candidate, Senator Robert F. Kennedy, and civil rights leader, Martin Luther King, were on everybody's mind, and because of the ongoing Vietnam war, the convention was very divisive.

Hubert Humphrey, Johnson's vice president from Minnesota had won the most votes n the primaries, but after leading Democratic presidential candidate, **Robert Kennedy**, was assassinated, Senator **Eugene McCarthy**, an antiwar candidate from Minnesota, began to get a lot of votes.

Despite the divisive nature of the convention, Humphrey easily won the vote for nomination. Surprisingly, instead of picking a Southerner as his running mate, he picked **Edmund Muskie**, U.S. Senator from Maine.

The 1968 presidential election took place in an atmosphere of ongoing antiwar protests. Although Nixon worked hard to get southern votes by appealing to conservatives, the segregationist Alabama Governor **George Wallace** managed to get himself on the ballot in the southern states as the presidential nominee of the **American Independent Party**. He chose the outspokenly militaristic Air Force General **Curtis LeMay** as his running mate.

Wallace's main election strategy was to try to get enough Electoral College votes in southern states to send the decision to the U.S. House of Representatives. He aggressively campaigned against the anti-segregation policies of Johnson and his vice president, Hubert Humphrey.

Wallace pledged an immediate withdrawal of U.S. troops from Vietnam. He made sure nobody thought he supported the antiwar protesters. Far from it; he said he was simply against the waste of money and lives in a pointless war in faraway Asia (which, of course, was exactly what most of the antiwar protesters were saying).

During the election, his running mate Curtis LeMay got a lot of attention by saying he did not fear using nuclear weapons in the fight against communism. He was widely quoted when he said the U.S. had the capability to **bomb Vietnam "back into the stone age."**

In the general election, Nixon's "southern strategy" failed to win very many southern states, mainly because of the strong showing of third-party candidate, George Wallace. But Nixon was able to get enough votes in the Midwest and West to win the election, even squeaking out a win in his usually-Democratic home state of California.

The national popular vote was one of the closest ever, 43.42% of the popular vote going to Nixon and 42.72% going to Humphrey. 31,783,783 votes were cast for Nixon, 31,271,839 went to Humphrey, and 9,901,118 went to Wallace. In the Electoral College, Nixon won 301 votes to Humphrey's 191.

Nixon's seemingly contradictory message of being *for* the war and against the antiwar protesters, and at the same time promising to somehow *end* the war with honor, had resonated with the American people.

Many observers felt Humphrey had lost a lot of votes because he didn't try hard enough to dissociate himself from Johnson's failed Vietnam policy. In addition, he had failed to follow through with the Democrat's "southern strategy" to win votes in South by supporting some of their demands.

With two Northerners running on the Democratic ticket, **Wallace** was able to get 46 Electoral College votes in the South. His strategy of getting enough electoral votes to deny either Nixon or Humphrey the majority and send the decision to the House of Representatives failed, but it would have worked if Humphrey could have accumulated more votes in the West and in the South to make the race closer.

To his credit, Humphrey refused to pander to the South by playing down his plan to pass more civil rights legislation, and he also refused to select a vice presidential candidate from the South. Those changes in strategy might have been enough to take at least some of Wallace's votes in the South and give Humphrey the win (in Georgia, for example, Humphrey lost to Nixon by only 45,671 vote while Wallace got 535,550 votes there). If Humphrey could had won a few of the southern states the Democrats had always won, he would have won the presidency. Wallace's role as a spoiler shows that a third-party candidate can have a dramatic effect on the outcome of the presidential race. As we shall see when we look at the presidential election of 2000, a third-party candidate can even deny the presidency to the popular vote winner.

COMMENT:

It didn't take Nixon long to grab hold of the same "**Vietnam tar baby**" that had ruined Johnson's presidency. By the time Nixon entered the White House, over 500,000 troops were stationed in Vietnam and **American soldiers were dying at the rate of 1200 a month there**. With the antiwar protests mounting and public opinion turning against the war, many expected Nixon to began to de-escalate U.S. involvement in Vietnam. But he did not. In fact, he escalated it.

The new Secretary of State, Henry Kissinger had convinced Nixon that the war was not "winnable" in the traditional sense, but Nixon knew withdrawal would be political suicide. He had been elected to "win" the war in Vietnam and to win it "with honor." That meant military victory in Vietnam was mandatory.

Nixon and Kissinger came up with a two part strategy: first, they would build up South Vietnam's military to get them to take over more of the actual combat. and secondly, Nixon would order an increase in the intensity of the war in hopes it would bring the North Vietnamese to the bargaining table.

Nixon ordered increased bombing of North Vietnam, including civilian areas. And he **ordered U.S. troops into the neighboring neutral countries** of Cambodia and Laos.

Meanwhile, at home, Nixon tried to paint anti-war groups as supporters of Communism. Even as the antiwar protests grew, he tried to appeal to the "silent majority," the majority of Americans he said were quietly supporting what he was doing in Vietnam. He tried to paint anyone who disagreed with him as radical communist sympathizers. He also railed against the "liberal media," saying most of their news items about him were distorted, manufactured attempts to discredit him.

Meanwhile, the antiwar protests increased. In response to the protests at Kent State University in Ohio, the governor of Ohio, James Rhodes, sent in the National Guard with live ammunition in their rifles. On Monday, May 4, 1970, members of the National Guard fired into a crowd of students. Thirteen students were hit, and four died. Some of the students who were killed were shot intentionally as they tried to run away, but other students were killed some distance away as they were walking to their classes.

When the details of the killings at Kent State were reported, many American Universities were shut down in sympathy.

Even though a presidential commission harshly criticized the guardsmen, concluding that "the indiscriminate firing of rifles into a crowd of students and the deaths that followed were unnecessary, unwarranted, and inexcusable," the killings dramatically increased the popularity of Governor Rhodes in Ohio and helped rejuvenate his flagging campaign for reelection. It was a clear indication of how divided the country had become during Nixon's presidency.

Nixon's more aggressive approach to the war in Vietnam was somewhat discredited in 1970 when news leaked out that the Army had been covering up massacres of Vietnamese civilians. It was learned that the military had successfully hushed up a U.S. Army massacre of 504 Vietnamese women, children, and old men in a village called My Lai. The massacre had taken place in the spring of 1968 and had been systematically covered up by the Army brass at all levels of command. Later interviews with some of the soldiers present at the massacre said they had been under orders to kill everybody in the village as part of a new "search and destroy" approach to the war. They said the mission was not an unusual one and that such things had been going on for some time. They said that at My Lai, in addition to the murders, rapes and torturing had taken place, and that there had been some mutilation of the civilian's bodies in revenge for American soldiers that had been killed or wounded over the preceding months.

Although the details of the mission were well known (several officers where on the ground during the massacre, and Colonel Oran K. Henderson, the brigade commander who had ordered the attack, observed it all from a helicopter hovering over the village), no action had been taken against the soldiers involved. On the contrary, everyone involved had been told to keep quiet about it.

Two and a years later, in November of 1970, a military trial brought criminal charges against 26 US soldiers who had been involved in the My Lai massacre. By the time the trial was over, all of the charges had been dropped. Only one officer, Second Lieutenant William Calley, a platoon leader, was found guilty. He was convicted of the premeditated murder of 22 Vietnamese civilians, even though he said he was only following direct orders that had been given to him by his superiors.

He was given a life sentence, but the next day, President Richard Nixon canceled the sentence and ordered Calley to be held under house arrest at Fort Benning.

While today we might think that the news that soldiers in Vietnam had been torturing, raping, and killing Vietnamese women and children would lead to public outrage, many rallied to the defense of the soldiers who had participated in the massacre. It was an indication of how divided the country was at that time. Some people were upset to learn there was an Army policy to cover up such occurrences, but at that time, it didn't seem to damage either the Army's credibility or Nixon's. approach to the war. Indiana's governor asked that all state flags to be flown at half-staff in support of Calley and his men. The governors of Utah and Mississippi came out publicly in support of Calley, and against his sentencing. The state legislatures of Arkansas, Kansas, Texas, New Jersey, and South Carolina voted to request clemency for Calley. Alabama's governor George Wallace visited Calley to express his support, and he formally requested that Nixon pardon Calley.

Calley stayed in his personal quarters at For Benning for three and a half years until President Nixon quietly arranged a pardon for him.

The Presidential Election of 1972

In 1972, it was clear that once again, the election was going to take place while the war in Vietnam dragged on.

In the Republican primaries, Nixon's only serious competition came from Congressman Pete McCloskey of California who ran as an antiwar candidate. At the Republican national convention presidential nominating convention, Nixon won easily.

The Democratic race was wide open with fifteen men and two women declaring their candidacy. They were (in alphabetical order):

Shirley Chisholm, U.S. Representative from New York.
Walter Fauntroy, U.S. Representative from Washington, D.C.
Fred Harris, U.S. Senator from Oklahoma.
Vance Hartke, U.S. Senator from Indiana
Hubert Humphrey, U.S. Senator from Minnesota, former VP.
Henry M. Jackson, U.S. Senator from Washington.
John Lindsay, Mayor of New York City, New York
Eugene J. McCarthy, former U.S. Senator from Minnesota
George McGovern, U.S. Senator from South Dakota
Wilbur Mills, U.S. Representative from Arkansa
Patsy Mink, U.S. representative from Hawaii
Edmund Muskie, U.S. Senator from Maine
Terry Sanford, former governor of North Carolina
George Wallace, Governor of Alabama
Sam Yorty, former U.S. Representative from California

The 1972 election also saw the emergence of several third party candidates vying for the presidency. Conservative U.S. Congressman **John G. Schmitz**, a member of the ultra-conservative **John Birch Society**, ran as a representative of the **American Party**, the party that George Wallace had run on in 1968. Schmitz got onto the ballot in 32 states and received 1,099,482 votes, but he won no Electoral College votes.

Linda Jenness was nominated by the **Socialist Workers Party**, with Andrew Pulley as her running-mate.

Benjamin Spock was nominated by the **People's Party**.

1972 was the first time the **Libertarian Party** fielded a candidate. They nominated **John Hospers**, but he was only able to get on the presidential ballot in Colorado and Washington (each state has their own rules about how to get on the presidential ballot, and Colorado and Washington are among the easiest.) Hospers received only 3,573 votes, but he did get one Electoral College vote in Virginia from a **"faithless elector."**

COMMENT:

The term **"faithless elector"** refers to a member of a state's Electoral College who does not vote for the presidential candidate who won the state's popular vote. As stated very specifically in the U.S. Constitution, **members of the Electoral College are not required to vote for the candidate that wins the popular vote**.

It might seem surprising that the framers of the Constitution of this nation *did not even suggest* that members of the Electoral College should vote for the winner of the popular vote. At the time, they wanted the electors to have that freedom in case **the people voted for "the wrong person."** By freeing members of the Electoral College to vote for anyone they chose to, *even if that person was not a candidate,* they assured that political leaders in the states would have the final say about who got to be president.

Faithless electors have never overturned an election, but over the years, there have been many who tried. Below is a brief description of each incident.

In 1796, Samuel Miles, an Federalist elector from Pennsylvania, refused to vote for the winner of the popular vote, Federalist candidate John Adams. Instead, he voted for Thomas Jefferson, the Democratic-Republican candidate. The Electoral College voting was so close, that had only a few more Federalist electors done the same thing, it would have changed the outcome of the election.

In 1808, six Democratic-Republican electors refused to support James Madison, their party's candidate for president, and instead, voted for George Clinton, the Democratic-Republican candidate for vie president.

In 1812, three Federalist electors refused to vote for the Federalist vice presidential candidate Jared Ingersoll. Instead, they voted for Elbridge Gerry, the vice presidential candidate from the opposing Democratic-Republican Party.

In 1820, James Monroe would have received all of the Electoral College votes if William Plummer, the governor of New Hampshire and a Democratic-Republican elector hadn't decided at the last minute to cast his vote for his friend, John Quincy Adams even though Adams was not a candidate in the 1820 election. Supposedly, Plummer was protesting against the "wasteful extravagance" of the Monroe Administration and used his Electoral College vote to bring attention to the issue. He also voted against Daniel D. Tompkins, Monroe's vice presidential choice, saying the man did "not have the weight of character which that office requires."

In 1828, seven of the nine electors from Georgia refused to vote for Andrew Jackson's choice for vice president, John Calhoun. Instead, they voted for William Smith, a senator from South Carolina who was a vocal opponent of Calhoun. (In 1837, President Andrew Jackson nominated Smith to the Supreme Court, but he declined the honor.)

1832 saw the largest rebellion of electors in history. Thirty-two electors from Pennsylvania and Maryland refused to vote for the presidential candidate that had won the popular vote. Two Republican Party electors from Maryland refused to vote for anyone rather than cast their votes for Henry Clay, the candidate who had won their state. In Pennsylvania , all 30 electors refused to vote for vice presidential candidate, **Martin Van Buren**, even though he had won the popular vote. Instead, they voted for **William Wilkins**, the senator from their home state of Pennsylvania. Andrew Jackson and Martin Van Buren won anyhow.

1836 saw something happen in the Electoral College that changed the outcome of the 1836 election and could have set a precedent that would change all future presidential elections: some electors refused to vote for the candidate that won the popular vote just because they didn't like his personal behavior. Twenty-three Democratic electors from Virginia refused to cast their votes for the winning Democratic vice president, Richard M. Johnson of Kentucky, because they had learned he was involved in a sexual relationship with an African-American woman. Johnson caused much consternation when he openly admitted he was the father of one of his slave's children. Furthermore, after that slave woman died, he took up sexual relationships with other female slaves, and he was not afraid to tell everybody about it.

With the loss of those 23 votes, there was no majority in the Electoral College, and as specified in the U.S. Constitution, the decision about who would be vice president was sent to the U.S. Senate. In the Senate, with little debate, the senators voted strictly along party lines to name Johnson vice president.

An unusual situation occurred in **1872. Sixty-three of the sixty-six Democratic electors** who were from states Horace Greeley had won voted for somebody else because Greeley had died between the time the election was held and when the Electoral College met. This was something the founding father hadn't considered when they created the Electoral College system. Seventeen of the Greeley electors chose to cast no vote at all, but the other 46 electors voted for whoever they liked personally. They voted for four different candidates for president, and eight different candidates for vice president. However, three of the electors followed what they saw as their duty and voted for the dead man. These votes were later disallowed by Congress, but it is not clear under what authority they disallowed the votes for Greeley because there is no provision in the Electoral College section of the Constitution specifying how such a situation should be dealt with.

As described earlier, the **presidential election of 1876** was the only election in which **Samuel J. Tilden, the candidate that won both the popular vote and the Electoral College vote did not get to be president**. A special Congressional commission, created after considerable contention, voted strictly along party lines to **invalidate many of the Electoral College votes from the South** due to perceived voter fraud. The commission declared the Republican, Rutherford B. Hayes, the Electoral College winner by one vote. Again, it is not clear under what authority they disallowed the Electoral College votes for Tilden. The Electoral College section of the Constitution does not mention any possible circumstance in which the winner of the Electoral College vote can be denied the presidency.

In 1896, four electors, unhappy with their winning vice presidential candidate, Thomas E. Watson, switched their votes to a different vice presidential candidate, Arthur Sewall from Maine.

In 1948, Preston Parks, a southern Democratic elector from Tennessee, refused to cast his vote for the Democratic winner, Harry S. Truman. Instead, he cast his vote for Strom Thurmond, the segregationist States' Rights candidate. It was a remarkable moment in Electoral College history because it showed that an elector could go so far as to vote for *the opponent* of the winner of the popular vote if the elector had a personal disagreement with the policies of the winner. Strom Thurmond ended up getting 39 Electoral College votes, all from southern electors.

In 1956, a southern Democratic elector, **W.F. Turner from Alabama**, voted for his friend, Walter Burgwyn Jones, a U.S. congressman from Alabama (who was not a candidate of any party). The elector didn't like Adlai Stevenson, the winner of the popular vote in Alabama, so he refused to vote for him.

In 1960, one elector planned a revolt that showed the danger of letting a few selected individuals decide who the nation's president would be. **Republican elector, Henry D. Irwin**, from Oklahoma, refused to vote for Richard Nixon, the candidate that had won his state. He simply said he "could not stomach" Nixon. But he went further, he tried to get all the other electors to reject both Nixon and Kennedy and vote instead for two of the most conservative members of the Senate, **Harry Byrd** of Virginia and **Barry Goldwater** of Arizona. He secretly tried to arrange a revolt among the southern electors, but in the end, the other electors were not willing to go along with his plan (fourteen *unpledged* electors from Mississippi and Alabama *did* cast their presidential votes for Harry Byrd). Although Irwin's plan failed, it did show what could happen if enough of the Electoral College members decided to get together and elect their own preferred candidate. If that happened, according to the wording of the Electoral College section of the Constitution, **there is nothing anyone could do about it**.

In **1968, Republican elector Dr. Lloyd W. Bailey of North Carolina** refused to vote for Richard Nixon (because he had appointed Henry Kissinger) and instead voted for George Wallace. Dr. Bailey pointed out (accurately) that the U.S. Constitution said nothing about him having to vote for the candidate who won his state. He also pointed out (accurately) that George Wallace had won his home district and that before the winner-take-all system had been instituted he would have been obliged to vote for Wallace.

In **1972, Republican elector Roger L. MacBride from Virginia** refused to cast his electoral vote for Richard Nixon, and instead voted for John Hospers, the Libertarian Presidential candidate. He also voted for the Libertarian vice presidential candidate, Toni Nathan, making her the first woman ever to receive an Electoral vote.

In **1976, Republican elector Mike Padden, a lawyer from Washington** refused to vote for the winner of his state, Gerald Ford, and instead voted for Ronald Reagan (who was not a candidate at that time).

In **1988, Democratic elector Margaret Leach from West Virginia** was shocked when she learned members of the Electoral College were not required to vote for the candidates they were pledged to. She decided to draw attention to this ridiculous situation by switching her votes for president and vice president. She cast her vote for Bentsen for president and Dukakis for vice president and she tried to get the other electors to do the same in order to show the citizens of the United States what was possible with the nonsensical Electoral College system in place. But she was unable to convince any of the others to do what she had done.

In **2000, Democratic elector Barbara Lett-Simmons from the District of Columbia** withheld her vote that was pledged to Al Gore. She **refused to cast any vote at all.** She intended it as a protest against the lack of Congressional representation for the citizens of Washington, DC.

In 2004, in a secret ballot, **a Minnesota elector cast a ballot for John Edwards instead of the winner of the state,** John Kerry. No one knows who it was or why he or she did it.

Today, 29 states and the District of Columbia have passed laws that impose penalties on electors who do not cast their vote for the presidential candidate that wins the popular vote in their state. That means there are **21 states that today still do not even attempt to exert any kind of legal control over how their electors vote.**

So far, it is unclear if laws that attempt to control how a member of the Electoral College votes are constitutional. Most historians believe the wording of the Electoral College section of the Constitution is no accident; the founding father wanted to be sure the electors *did* have a free rein to vote for whoever they wanted.

As the 1972 presidential election neared, it was clear that if Nixon was to win reelection, he was going to have to show progress was being made in Vietnam. The public's perception of the war in Vietnam was constantly growing less favorable. They were ready for the war to be over.

As a result, Nixon's campaign message was twofold: first, he tried to convince the American public that the war was going well; second, he had to convince them that his strategy was working to the degree that the war would soon be over, meaning we would be able to get out of the Vietnam mess with some semblance of honor.

Peace talks were still going on in Paris, and just before the election, Henry Kissinger returned to the United States and went before the press to announce that "peace is at hand."

Nixon's message was also positive. He said the U.S. had never lost a war, and "we are not going to lose this one."

Nixon's plan worked. Although the public was fed up with the war in Vietnam, and there were stories being printed in the newspapers about a secret group of "dirty trick's" anti-Democrat operatives that were said to be connected to the White House, Nixon still had plenty of support in the country (the silent majority?). He won the Electoral College vote in every state except Massachusetts.

However, the popular vote was close in some states. For example, Michigan cast 1,961,721 votes for Nixon and 1,459,435 votes for McGovern, and in Wisconsin Nixon only won by 179,256 votes.

When Nixon won the South in 1972, it was **the first time in U.S. history a Republican had won every single southern state**. After 132 years, it appeared the South had finally forgiven the Republicans for electing Lincoln.

It was clear that with the Republicans finally gaining the upper hand in the South, they would have a much greater chance of winning the presidency in future elections, and that was the way it turned out.

Four out of the next five presidents (all except for Ronald Reagan, the very conservative candidate from California), were Southerners. Jimmy Carter was from Georgia, George H. W. Bush was from Texas, Bill Clinton was from Arkansas, and George W. Bush was from Texas.

COMMENT:

The **Paris Peace Accords** were signed in January of 1973. Nixon had ordered intense bombing of civilian areas of North Vietnam in order to force North Vietnam to the peace table, but a much more important concession was that America was ready to leave Vietnam to the Vietnamese. The country would remain divided. The U.S. would train and equip the South Vietnamese Army, but the U.S. military would leave the country.

Although the peace accords ended America's involvement in the war, it didn't end the war. Nixon ordered a "Vietnamization" of the war, a program of training and equipping the Army of the public of Viet Nam (ARVN) to be sure they could hold South Vietnam without the presence of U.S. troops.

The Vietnamization program was a complete failure. When the North Vietnamese again invaded the south, the South Vietnamese military was unable to hold them back.

President Nixon had said publicly that if the North Vietnamese invaded South Vietnam again, the United States would again intervene. But when his Secretary of Defense, James R. Schlesinger, stated that he was ready to recommend resumption of the U.S. bombing of North Vietnam, the U.S. Senate quickly passed the **Case-Church Amendment** to prohibit any more direct U.S. involvement in Vietnam.

It could be said that the U.S. role in the Vietnam war began with secret CIA involvement, and ended when the CIA left. Near the end of April, 1975, the last CIA station personnel in Saigon were airlifted off of the roof of the American Embassy by helicopters belonging to Air America , a small airline secretly owned by the CIA.

Chapter Twelve
Secret Presidential Power

As Nixon was winning the presidency in 1972, the American public had just started hearing about a secret security group that was said to be working out of the White House. Soon after the election, more information about the group was beginning to come to light. Known as the **White House plumbers,** the secret group was said to be investigating leaks and other security matters, but when the public found out what the group was really up to, and it would lead to Nixon being the first and only president in U.S. history to be forced to resign the office.

COMMENT:

As the campaigning for the presidential election of 1972 was taking place, members of Nixon's **White House plumbers** group were trying to find out what the Democratic strategy for the election was. On the night of June 17, 1972, they broke into the Democratic National Committee (DNC) headquarters in the **Watergate** building in Washington, D.C. They looked for information about Democratic strategy, and they placed wiretaps in the DNC offices.

A security guard noticed tape on a door that was being used to keep the door from locking. He called the police, and five men, Bernard Barker, Virgilio González, Eugenio Martínez, James McCord, and Frank Sturgis, were caught inside the Democratic National Committee offices and arrested.

As soon as Nixon found out about the arrests, he and his Attorney General John Mitchell began a frantic cover-up to keep the American public from finding out what was really behind the break-in.

Nixon's **presidential Counsel John Dean**, spearheaded the cover-up effort, and at first, Nixon was confident they would be able to distance themselves from it.

But two reporters from the **Washington Post** newspaper, **Bob Woodward and Carl Bernstein**, kept digging and eventually managed to contact an informant who gave them information implicating the president. The two reporters refused to name their informant. They said the informant was known only by the code name, "**Deep Throat**" (many years later the informant was revealed to be Federal Bureau of Investigation Associate Director Mark Felt).

Woodward and Bernstein were able to trace money that had paid to the Watergate burglars. It turned out to be money that had been donated to the president's reelection effort.

Piece by piece, Woodward, Bernstein, and other reporters ferreted out more information about the White House plumbers group. Eventually, all five Watergate burglars were tied directly or indirectly to the Nixon's reelection committee.

On October 10, 1972, a month before the election, Woodward and Bernstein reported that fact in a front page story in the Washington Post. But people either didn't believe the story, or they didn't care. The polls still showed Nixon had plenty of support.

Only one week before the 1972 election, it was revealed that **Attorney General John Mitchell had controlled a secret Republican fund** used to finance intelligence-gathering against the Democrats. Although there were suspicions that Nixon himself was involved, the election results showed the Republicans were still solidly behind him.

Despite intense efforts on the part of the recently reelected president to cover up the whole mess, information continued to come out. Nevertheless, Nixon and other high ranking officials in his administration continued to deny they knew anything about it.

In March of 1973, five months after Nixon had been elected with an overwhelming Electoral College majority, his attorney, John Dean, fearing a prison sentence for himself, began cooperating with the U.S. Attorney's office. He implicated several of Nixon's aides. Nixon continued to deny any knowledge of the plumbers or the cover-up.

In May of 1973, **the U.S. Senate formed a committee to investigate** the whole Watergate affair. The hearings were televised live nationally, and the entire country watched with rapt attention as the story unfolded through the testimony of John Dean and other members of Nixon's inner circle.

One bit of tantalizing information Dean revealed to the committee was that Nixon secretly audio taped all of his meetings. The committee asked Nixon to turn over the tapes, but he refused. It took a series of court battles that eventually led to a decision by the U.S. Supreme Court that he had to comply with the request and turn over transcripts of the tapes. Although forensic analyses of the tapes showed that some conversations had been intentionally erased, they did reveal that Nixon was aware of hush payment to some of the Watergate defendants. The tapes also revealed that Nixon tried to get the CIA to claim that the Watergate break-in was part of a national security investigation.

In July, the House filed **articles of impeachment against Nixon**, citing three articles: 1) obstruction of justice, 2) abuse of power, and 3) contempt of Congress.

At first, some Congressional Republicans stood firm in their support of Nixon, but when more tapes came to light showing how actively Nixon was involved in the cover-up, they too indicated they would be forced to vote for impeachment.

When Nixon heard that even the Republicans in Congress were abandoning him, he went on TV to announce he was resigning the presidency. He left the White House the next day. He was **the first any only U.S. President ever to resign the office**.

Vice President Gerald Ford succeeded him and soon **granted Nixon a full pardon for any crimes he might have committed while president.** Although, with a presidential pardon in hand, Nixon himself could not be prosecuted, a total of 25 officials from the Nixon administration, **including four cabinet members**, were eventually convicted and imprisoned.

The Presidential Election of 1976

After Nixon resigned, **Gerald Ford** served out the remainder of the presidential term and ran for reelection in **1976**.

In 1976, more and more people were aspiring to be president. Fifteen candidates competed in the Democratic primaries, including governors, senators, U.S. representatives, an ambassador, and a housewife. They were (in alphabetical order):

Robert Byrd, U.S. senator from West Virginia
Birch Bayh, U.S. senator from Indiana
Lloyd Bentsen, U.S. senator from Texas
Jerry Brown, governor of California
Jimmy Carter, former governor of Georgia
Frank Church, U.S. senator from Idaho
Walter Fauntroy, U.S. representative from Washington, D.C.
Fred R. Harris, former U.S. senator from Oklahoma
Henry M. Jackson, U.S. senator from Washington
Ellen McCormack, a housewife from New York
Terry Sanford, former governor of North Carolina
Milton Shapp, governor of Pennsylvania
Sargent Shriver, former U.S. ambassador to France from
     Maryland
Morris Udall, U.S. representative from Arizona
George Wallace, governor of Alabama

As the 1976 primaries went on, it became clear that **Jimmy Carter**, the former governor of Georgia was going to prevail. He was nominated at the Democratic nominating convention and went on to mount an effective campaign as an outsider who would go to Washington to change the kind of politics Nixon had been engaged in.

In the 1976 general election, Carter and his running mate, Walter Mondale from Minnesota, won all the southern states except Virginia (where they lost by only 22,658 votes).

Ford won most of the midwestern and western states, but his controversial pardon of Nixon hurt him the East.

The popular vote was fairly close with 40,831,881 votes going to Carter and 39,148,634 votes to Ford. The Electoral College vote was 297 for Carter and 240 for Ford.

Eugene McCarthy, a former Democratic senator from Minnesota known for his anti-Vietnam position ran as an independent and got 756,631 popular votes, but he didn't win any electoral votes.

The Presidential Election of 1980

As the 1980 presidential election season began, the American people were dismayed over the slow economy, and they were upset about the taking of American hostages in Iran, an incident that became known as the **Iran Hostage Crisis**.

Many were also upset with Carter's decision not to allow U.S. athletes to compete in the 1980 Olympics in Moscow. It was his way of protesting the Soviet invasion of Afghanistan, but many felt the international Olympic movement was a venue to honor the world's best athletes and not a place for political statements. They felt if President Carter's Olympic boycott was allowed to stand, other countries would retaliate and every Olympics would be marred by political posturing.

President **Jimmy Carter** led in most of the Democratic primaries, but **Senator Edward M. (Ted) Kennedy** of Massachusetts was making a strong showing.

By the time the Democratic national presidential nominating convention came around, Carter had enough votes to win, but a strong anti-Carter mood on the convention floor resulted in a last minute "draft Muskie" movement to replace Carter with Secretary of State **Edmund Muskie** from Maine. It failed and Carter was nominated.

COMMENT:

The **Iranian Hostage Crisis** came about in the fall of 1979 after a group of Islamist students and militant revolutionaries took over the American embassy in Tehran.

The revolutionaries were involved in a power struggle with Mohammad Rezā Shāh Pahlavī, **the Shah of Iran** who was supported by the United States as part of **the cold war** with Russia. With the support of Revolutionary leader Ayatollah Ruhollah Khomeini, the militants captured American citizens who had been in the embassy and held them as hostages.

As the months went by, President Carter came under increasing criticism for not doing something about it. Finally, Carter approved a rescue mission code named **Operation Eagle**. The plan was to use helicopters and U.S. Army Delta Force troops to fly into Iran and rescue the hostages, but some of the helicopters suffered mechanical problems and the mission was called off. Unfortunately, as one of the helicopters was being refueled, it collided with the refueling tanker aircraft. The helicopter crashed and soldiers were killed.

More than a year passed before the new government of Iran, now under the control of Ayatollah Ruhollah Khomeini, agreed to release the hostages if the U.S. would agree to release several billion dollars of Iranian assets that had been frozen in American banks when the hostages were first taken. President Carter was secretly working with various international banks to make the deal come about, but it took so long to finalize the details that by the time the hostages were flown out of Iran, Carter had already been defeated by Ronald Reagan. It was the new president that welcomed the hostages home.

The early 1980 Republican primaries indicated that their nominee would likely be former California Governor Ronald Reagan. Reagan was fairly well known outside of California because before being elected governor, he had been a movie actor and had also appeared in many TV commercials.

Baring any unexpected developments, Reagan was sure to win the Republican nomination at the Republican nominating convention. Nevertheless, there were eight others who opposed him They were (in alphabetical order):

John B. Anderson, U.S. Representative from Illinois

Howard Baker, U.S. senator from Tennessee

George H. W. Bush of Texas, U.S. representative and former CIA director

John Connally, former governor of Texas

Phil Crane, U.S. representative from Illinois

Bob Dole, U.S. senator from Kansas

Harold Stassen, former governor of Minnesota

Lowell Weicker, U.S. senator from Connecticut

Reagan won the nomination and selected one of his opponents, **George H. W. Bush** of Texas as his running mate.

In the general election, Reagan based his campaign on **"conservative values,"** giving Carter ammunition for his accusations that Reagan was a dangerous right wing radical who would take the country down the wrong path.

Although Ronald Reagan had previously been a registered Democrat who supported Roosevelt's very liberal **"New Deal"** policies, his two terms in office as California's Republican governor established his credentials as a **conservative**.

His tenure as California's governor took place during a time of **great dissonance in the state over the Vietnam War**. As soon as he was elected governor, Reagan showed that he was going to support the conservative side on most issues. He got a lot of support from conservatives when he promised to "crack down" on student anti-war protests in all California state universities. (He called the student protesters "welfare bums.")

Because of Reagan's aggressive tactics against student protesters, there was a recall effort mounted against him. The recall effort failed, and Reagan took that as a sign that his policies had the support of the people.

When, despite his efforts, the anti-Vietnam protests continued to grow at California state universities, Reagan began using the state police against the protesters. When a large **"people's protest"** was staged at the University of California campus in Berkeley, he called in state National Guard troops. The National Guard occupied the area of the city around the campus for two weeks. When one student, James Rector, was killed by police gunfire, Reagan's response was, "If it takes a bloodbath, let's get it over with. No more appeasement."

COMMENT:

It was later learned that Reagan had been secretly working as an informer for the FBI since his days as head of the Hollywood Screen Actors Guild. Because of Reagan's aggressive efforts to root out Communists from the Screen Actors Guild and from California universities, J. Edgar Hoover, the head of the FBI, became a strong Reagan supporter. Hoover used the FBI's resources to help Reagan politically whenever he could, and even assigned FBI agents to help Reagan with some of his personal family matters.

Another hotly debated national issue that arose during Reagan's term as governor was the national debate about the legalization of abortion. The liberal California State Legislature passed a bill legalizing abortion in California and sent it to Reagan for his signature. After many days of indecision, he signed it (later, during his run for the presidency, he would say he regretted signing it).

The election of 1980 was not even close. Although President Carter had a big lead in the polls only a few weeks before the election, radicals in Iran were still holding U.S. citizens as hostages. Reagan relentlessly attacked Carter's handling of the Iran hostage situation, and in the end, he won easily.

Part of Carter's problem was that although he was a Southerner, the South was now firmly in the Republican camp. Reagan won every southern state except Alabama (where he lost by only 17,462 votes). Carter even lost his home state of Arkansas, although by only 5,123 votes.

Reagan's Electoral College win of 489 to 49 was the largest in U.S. history for a candidate running against an incumbent.

> **COMMENT:**
>
> In the election campaign of 1980, Republican Congressman John B. Anderson of Illinois managed to get himself on the ballot in many states, running as an independent. However, President Carter refused to participate in debates with him. Reagan did debate Anderson, and most observers felt Anderson had done very well against the polished actor, Reagan. In the general election, Anderson got 5,719,850 votes but won no electoral votes.

The Presidential Election of 1984

In the presidential election of 1984, Reagan ran for reelection, but being **the oldest president in U.S. history**, there were questions about whether he should be elected for another term. Nevertheless, he dominated the primaries and easily won the nomination at the Republican presidential nominating convention.

After Senator Ted Kennedy again declined to run for president, the Democratic primaries indicated the nomination would come down to three candidates, former vice president, **Walter Mondale** of Minnesota, Senator **Gary Hart** of Colorado, and civil rights leader **Jesse Jackson** of Illinois.

At the Democratic nominating convention, Mondale won and chose New York Congresswoman Geraldine Ferraro as his running mate. It was the first time a woman had been on the ticket of any major political party. The Democrats hoped she would attract the women's vote.

Mondale and Ferraro immediately began an attack on Reagan's so-called conservative values, saying they were intended to use the threat of communism to scare Americans into going along with extreme government policy. They also said his so-called anti-socialist economic policies were being used to turn Americans against the poor and minorities.

The Reagan campaign focused mostly on his "cold war" foreign policy and on his approach to American economics that had became known as "**Reaganomics**." Reaganomics was the idea that if you get rid of business regulations and cut taxes on the rich, the resulting benefits to the most wealthy would "trickle down" to the middle class.

During the primaries, Reagan had little opposition, although another Republican candidate, George H. W. Bush, derided Reaganomics as **"voodoo economics."**

After the nominations, the nation tuned in to the televised debates. After the first debate, which was limited to domestic policy, most observers felt Reagan had done poorly against Mondale. Reagan seemed hesitant and at times confused. But in the second debate, which was about international policy and national defense, Reagan seemed much more confident.

Even as the debates were going on, the Reagan campaign was producing slick television ads that emphasized the threat from Russia and fostered a "peace through strength" approach to foreign policy. The ads said it was the only way to stop the spread of worldwide communism. These ads drew attention to how much Reagan had strengthened the U.S military during his first term.

COMMENT:

Reagan's cold war foreign policy of fighting communism on all fronts was quite vividly demonstrated in 1983 when a military coup in Granada, a small island off the coast of Venezuela, replaced the government with one that was sympathetic to Communist ideals. Reagan immediately sent in 7,000 troops consisting of ranger battalions and airborne paratroopers to depose the new Granada government.

Although most Americans supported the invasion as a necessary part of the fight against Communism, it was criticized by the United Kingdom, Canada and the United Nations General Assembly as "a flagrant violation of international law."

Reagan's anti-Communist campaign approach, plus his personal appeal, worked. He won the 1984 general and Electoral College elections easily. He even won 55 percent of the women's vote in the general election **despite the presence of a woman on the Democratic ticket**.

The Mondale-Ferraro ticket won only Mondale's home state of Minnesota and the District of Columbia.

Reagan was a popular president, but information began to leak out that he had created a special task force not unlike the one that had resulted in Nixon's resignation. Further investigation led to what is now known as the **Iran-Contra scandal** (sometimes referred to as **"Irangate"**). The question was, would it hurt Reagan's chances for reelection?

COMMENT:

The **Iran-Contra scandal** began when President Reagan created a secret organization known as "the Enterprise." It was originally created as a way to deal with Iran in order to gain the release of the hostages being held by terrorists in Lebanon.

The Enterprise group worked out a deal with the Iranian Army wherein the U.S. would sell weapons to Iran to help with their ongoing war with Iraq. In return, the Iranian Army would try to secure the release of the U.S. hostages being held there.

National Security Adviser Robert McFarlane told President Reagan about the potential deal, but they were stymied because there was an embargo against selling arms to Iran. Reagan wanted to go ahead with the deal anyhow. **Secretary of Defense Caspar Weinberger** and **Secretary of State George Shultz** opposed the deal, but McFarlane and **CIA director William Casey** supported it. With the backing of President Reagan, the plan was put into action.

The result was that arms, including thousands of missiles, were sent to Iran, and in exchange, a few hostages were released. Unfortunately, they were quickly replaced with new hostages. It appeared that Iran had discovered a way to get military arms from the U.S. - just take hostages and then trade them for weapons.

When the Lebanese newspaper, **Al-Shiraa**, printed an exposé of the deal in November of 1986, President Reagan went on TV to vehemently deny any such deal had been made.

A week later, he admitted the operation *had* occurred, but said it was definitely not an arms-for-hostages deal.

Polls taken at the time indicated most Americans **believed President Reagan was not telling the truth** about the deal. Although Reagan's popularity declined somewhat as more information about the arms for hostages deal came out, he still had plenty of support among Republicans. They felt that although what he had done might have been illegal, it had been done with good intentions.

That might have been the end of the affair, but it was soon discovered that eighteen million dollars out of the thirty million dollars the Iranians had paid for the American weapons had disappeared. A member of the National Security Council, **Lieutenant Colonel Oliver North**, admitted he had been diverting funds from the arms sales to **the Contras**, a group that was fighting against the Communist government in Nicaragua. Although direct support of the Contras was against U.S. law, Reagan was well known as a supporter of the Contras, calling them "the moral equivalent of our founding fathers." It was also revealed that North had been working with drug smugglers and with Panamanian dictator Manuel Noriega to assist the Contras. North said everything he had done had been done **with the full knowledge of National Security Adviser Admiral John Poindexter and, he assumed, with the full knowledge of President Reagan. Poindexter resigned and North was fired**, but Reagan continued to claim he didn't know anything about it.

To many members of the national media, the connection between the arms sale and the diversion of the money to the Reagan-supported Contra seemed too obvious. They hounded the president about it at every press conference, but Reagan continued to deny any knowledge of what his closest advisors were up to.

Some of Reagan's aides were tried and convicted, but when Reagan's vice president George H. W. Bush was elected in 1988, **he pardoned most of them**, including a pardon of Secretary of Defense Caspar W. Weinberger just days before he was to go to trial.

Oliver North was indicted on sixteen felony counts, but they were all later overturned.

Using the publicity he got during the Iran-Contra hearings, North ran for the U.S. senate in 1994 as a Republican against Democrat Charles Robb, son-in-law of President Lyndon B. Johnson. North was able to raise over twenty million dollars to fund his campaign, but he was still defeated.

Since then, North has been a regular commentator on the Fox News Channel and has written several best-selling books.

Chapter Thirteen
Foreign Wars and Presidential Scandal

The Presidential Election of 1988

The presidential election of 1988 saw Vice President **George H. W. Bush** winning **the Republican nomination** by promising to continue the policies of outgoing president Ronald Reagan. He chose Senator **Dan Quayle** from Indiana as his running mate.

With the Iran Contra scandal continuing to unfold, the Democrats were optimistic that they could take back the presidency in 1988. Due to the scandal, they had regained control of the senate after six years of Republican domination.

In 1988, a large number of candidates fought for the Democratic nomination. They were (in alphabetical order):

Douglas Applegate, U.S. Representative from Ohio.
Bruce Babbitt, former Governor of Arizona.
Joe Biden, U.S. Senator from Delaware.
David Duke from Louisiana.
Michael Dukakis, Governor of Massachusetts.
Al Gore, U.S. Senator from Tennessee.
Dick Gephardt, U.S. Representative from Missouri.
Gary Hart, former U.S. Senator from Colorado.
Jesse Jackson from Illinois.
Lyndon LaRouche from Virginia.
Andy Martin from Connecticut.
Paul Simon, U.S. Senator from Illinois.
James Traficant, U.S. Representative from Ohio.

At first, Gary Hart seemed to be the most likely nominee, but questions were raised about his extramarital affairs.

Senator Edward M. Kennedy of Massachusetts again decided against running in 1988, and Arkansas Governor Bill Clinton also declined to run.

Eventually, the convention nominated **Michael Dukakis,** the governor of Massachusetts. He chose U.S. Senator **Lloyd Bentsen** as his running mate.

The 1988 campaign was one of finger pointing. Bush said Dukakis was too liberal, and Dukakis said Bush was too conservative and too militaristic.

Dukakis tried to tie Bush to the Iran-Contra scandal, saying Bush's involvement in the sale of arms to Iran showed Bush had "failed the test of leadership."

In the general election, Bush won the popular vote by about seven million votes (out of ninety million votes cast). In the Electoral College vote, the margin was larger, 426 to 111.

The Republican candidate, Bush, won the South, as was becoming the trend, but he also won California and most of the midwestern and northern states. Those were states that the Democrats had counted on winning. (It was the last election in which the Republican candidate won California).

Libertarian Ron Paul from Texas and his running mate, **Andre V. Marrou** from Alaska were also on the ballot in many states. They gathered 431,750 votes nationwide, but no electoral votes.

At first, Bush was a popular president. But a 1990 jump in the price of oil tied to a brief war in **the Middle East** (now known as the **first Gulf War**), a weak economy, and **huge government budget deficits** hurt his popularity.

As the 1992 presidential elections approached, his chances of being reelected seemed in doubt.

COMMENT:

The **first Gulf War** was a military action waged by a UN-authorized coalition of forces against Iraq in response to Iraq's invasion of Kuwait.

In August of 1990, Iraqi troops invaded Kuwait with the intention of annexing the country. It was met by widespread condemnation and immediate economic sanctions against Iraq by some UN member nations.

President Bush sent American ships to the area and **deployed forces in Saudi Arabia** to gather near the Kuwait border. President Bush asked other countries to do the same. Military forces from Saudi Arabia, Britain, and Egypt responded and promised financial support.

Starting **in January of 1991, the U.S. began an aerial bombardment** on Iraqi positions, and much of the aerial attack was shown on American television.

Ground troops soon followed, and within a few days, the Iraqi forces had been pushed back into their own country. As the U.S. ground forces pushed into Iraq, the Iraqi military retreated. At that point, President Bush ordered a cease fire. The war had lasted only a few days, and some in the U.S. criticized the president for not continuing the war. However, both Bush and his Secretary of Defense, Dick Cheney, pointed out that they did not have a UN mandate to do more than push the Iraqis out of Kuwait. They felt further action would have made enemies of their allies in the area.

By the end of hostilities, it is estimated there were between 20,000 and 35,000 Iraq military fatalities plus many thousands of civilian deaths (one estimate put the number of civilian deaths as high as 100,000).

According to the U.S. Department of Defense, U.S. forces suffered 148 battle-related deaths, 35 of them from so-called "friendly fire" (killed by their own troops), and another 145 deaths in non-combat accidents.

The United Kingdom reported 47 deaths, 9 to friendly fire.

Other countries that were involved reported 37 deaths.

The Presidential Election of 1992

The presidential election of 1992 once again brought a third-party candidate to the fore.

President George H. W. Bush ran for reelection and was nominated by the **Republicans**. Although there was some discussion about replacing Dan Quayle as the vice presidential candidate, Bush again chose Quayle.

After a long and contentions primary season, the **Democrats** finally nominated popular Arkansas Governor Bill Clinton over Governor Jerry Brown of California, Senator Tom Harkin of Iowa, Senator Bob Kerrey of Nebraska, former Senator Eugene McCarthy, former Senator Paul Tsongas of Massachusetts, and Governor Douglas Wilder of Virginia.

Clinton chose Tennessee Senator Al Gore to be his running mate.

The surprise of 1992 was the candidacy of Texas billionaire Ross Perot. At one point during the campaign, **he was leading both Bush and Clinton in the national polls**. It seemed as if the public was ready to consider an outsider for president.

The Bush campaign chose a personal attack strategy. They accused Clinton of marital infidelity and draft dodging.

The **Clinton campaign** focused almost entirely on the economy and the fact that the Republicans had a long history of increasing the size of government and thereby increasing the national debt.

Political polling was getting ever more sophisticated, and the polls were indicating that Bush's personal attack strategy wasn't working. People were more concerned with their own pocketbooks.

Another problem for the Republicans was that the cold war was finally cooling down. After a political moderate, Mikhail Gorbachev, was named the General Secretary of the Communist Party of the Soviet Union in 1985, much of the Republican rhetoric about **the worldwide Communist threat** fell on deaf ears. By 1989, the Berlin Wall had come down and the phrase "Iron Curtain" was relegated to history. With no looming enemy abroad, all Bush had left to campaign on was his record, and many observers felt Bush's famous 1988 campaign promise of "Read my lips: no new taxes" hurt him in the 1992 election because he had in fact been forced to raise taxes as part of a compromise with Congress.

Midway through the 1992 race, Clinton was still leading in the polls, but when the presidential debates began, Ross Perot made some gains by attacking *both* Bush and Clinton.

Some felt Perot would pull votes away from Clinton, improving Bush's chances for reelection, but Perot was also talking about the poor economy and pointing out how much the Republicans were running up the national debt.

In the end, Clinton's message about the Republican's handling of the economy won out. Clinton won the popular election by 5,805,256 votes (out of 104,423,923 votes cast), but won the Electoral College vote even more convincingly, 370 to 168.

Perot managed to get 19,743,821 votes, but he wasn't able to win a single state and therefore didn't get any Electoral College votes. It seems Perot pulled votes away from *both* Clinton and Bush.

The Presidential Election of 1996

By the time the election of 1996 rolled around, Clinton was being credited with improving the economy, and he was reducing the national debt. He was also successful at keeping the U.S. out of any foreign wars. The absence of a Russian threat, meant he was able to cut some military expenditures which helped reduce the national debt even more.

As soon as President **Clinton announced that he would seek reelection in 1992**, the Republican began to attack his character. They began to criticize his "liberalism" even before they had selected a candidate.

No less than ten serious candidates **fought for the Republican presidential nomination** during the Republican primaries. They were (in alphabetical order):

Lamar Alexander, former governor of Tennessee.
Pat Buchanan from Virginia.
Bob Dole, U.S. Senator from Kansas.
Bob Dornan, U.S. Representative from California.
Steve Forbes, a wealthy publisher from New York.
Phil Gramm, U.S. Senator from Texas.
Alan Keyes, a former ambassador from Maryland.
Richard Lugar, U.S. Senator from Indiana.
Arlen Specter, U.S. Senator from Pennsylvania.
Pete Wilson, Governor of California.

Pat Buchanan, a well-known conservative, won some of the early Republican primaries, but eventually **Bob Dole** pulled ahead and was nominated as the Republican's 1992 presidential candidate. He chose **Jack Kemp,** a former congressman (and former professional football player) as his running mate.

As the campaign began, Ross Perot once again jumped into the race.

With no serious competition for the Democratic nomination, Clinton was able to get his campaign started early. Without meaningful primary opposition, he was able to focus on the general election early. He raised huge amounts of money and used it to mount a intensive TV campaign.

In order to secure the Republican nomination, Dole had to appeal to the more conservative elements of the Republican party, especially in the South. That gave Clinton the ammunition he needed to paint Dole as a right-winger who would cut popular social programs like Medicare and Social Security.

The relatively young and talkative Clinton came off well in the election debates. In contrast, Dole seemed much older and more hesitant.

Ross Perot's chances of winning any Electoral College votes were dashed when he was left out of the televised presidential debates. (He later sued, claiming an unfair lack of coverage by the TV networks, but his lawsuit was thrown out of court.)

In the 1996 general election, Clinton lost most of the South and the Midwest, but he was able to regain Democratic dominance in California and in the East. He won the popular vote by 8,201,370 votes and won the Electoral College vote 379 to 159.

In his second term, Clinton continued his policy of budget reductions and reduced military expenditures, but in 1998, there was talk on the internet that he was involved in a sexual relationship with a 22-year-old White House intern named Monica Lewinsky. At first Clinton denied the affair, but eventually admitted he had engaged in some sexual "fooling around" with Lewinsky.

The Republicans, who were in control of the House of Representatives at that time, impeached him for trying to cover up the affair.

Although a few past presidents have been threatened with impeachment, President Clinton was only the second president in the history of the United States to **actually be impeached** by the House of Representatives.

COMMENT:

The **Lewinsky scandal**, sometimes referred to as "**Monicagate**," came to light in the fall of 1997 when White House intern, **Monica Lewinsky**, confided to a coworker named **Linda Tripp** that she had been having a sexual affair with President Clinton.

Tripp reported it to **literary agent, Lucianne Goldberg**, who advised Tripp to engage Lewinsky in more conversations about it and secretly record whatever Lewinsky said.

When Tripp did that, Goldberg urged Tripp to take the tapes to **Kenneth Starr**. Starr had been appointed by President Reagan to a federal judgeship, but was at that time a private practice lawyer acting as an independent counsel to investigate some of President Clinton's past real estate investments.

Goldberg began speaking to reporters about the existence of the tapes, and in January of 1998, the Washington Post reported the accusations.

Clinton immediately denied having "sexual relations" with Miss Lewinsky.

His wife, Hillary Clinton, stood by her husband throughout the scandal, describing it as "a vast right-wing conspiracy that has been conspiring against my husband."

By the summer of that year, Lewinsky had been called before a grand jury and had received transactional immunity in exchange for her testimony. She told the grand jury about the affair, and later turned over a semen-stained dress to Starr as DNA evidence proving she was telling the truth.

When Clinton was called before the grand jury, he admitted he had had an "improper physical relationship" with Lewinsky that was "not appropriate." But he defended himself against the charge that he had lied about the affair when he said he had not had sexual relations with her by saying he had not understood that letting her perform oral sex on him could be included in the strict definition of "sexual relations." He said he had never been "the actor," in the affair and had never made physical contact with Lewinsky's "genitalia, anus, groin, breast, inner thigh, or buttocks."

That argument didn't carry much weight with the Republicans in the House of Representatives. They were in the majority and they initiated impeachment proceedings against him. Almost all of the Republicans in the House voted for the majority of the articles of impeachment, and four Democratic representatives from the South voted with them, as did Representative Paul McHale of Pennsylvania.

If a president is impeached by the House of Representatives it is sort of like being indicted for a crime; the "trial," if you want to think of it like that, takes place in the senate. It requires a two-thirds majority of the senators to remove a president from office.

After the senate "trial," 45 Republican senators voted guilty on the charge of perjury, and 55 senators (all of the Democrats and 10 of the Republicans) voted not guilty.

On the charge of obstruction of justice, 50 Republicans voted guilty; 45 Democrats and five Republicans voted not guilty. The vote did not meet the two-thirds majority requirement, so President Clinton was acquitted of all charges and was able to serve out the remainder of his second term in office.

Chapter Fourteen
The Electoral College System Fails Again

The Presidential Election of 2000

Now we come to the all important presidential election of 2000. I hope in the preceding pages I have clarified the complex and often unwieldy way presidents are elected in the United States. With that understanding in mind, let's examine closely the 2000 presidential election in order to understand how a candidate could win the popular vote by 543,895 votes and yet not get to be president.

After the revelation of President Clinton's sexual exploits in the White House and his impeachment for trying to deny it, many wondered how it would affect the Democratic party in the next election. Everybody knew **it would hurt the Democrats**, but no one knew if it would be enough to overcome the positive effect of the Democrats having been in power **during a time of peace with a good economy**.

Al Gore, Clinton's vice president took the position that the affair was behind us and that it had nothing to do with him. He ran for the nomination and won every single state primary election. He selected **Joseph I. Lieberman**, senator from Connecticut as his running mate. (Lieberman was the first observant Jew to be named on the ticket of any major party, and that fact was to have important ramifications in the election.)

The **Republican primaries** were wide open. There were no fewer than 13 candidates vying for the nomination. They were (in alphabetical order):

Lamar Alexander, former governor of Tennessee.
Gary Bauer, former Undersecretary of Education from Kentucky.
Pat Buchanan from Virginia.

George W. Bush, governor of Texas.

Herman Cain from Nebraska.

Elizabeth Dole, former Secretary of Labor from North Carolina.

Steve Forbes from New Jersey.

Orrin Hatch, U.S. Senator from Utah.

Alan Keyes, former U.S. ambassador from Maryland.

John Kasich, U.S. Representative from Ohio.

John McCain, U.S. Senator from Arizona.

Dan Quayle, former vice president from Indiana.

Robert C. Smith, U.S. Senator from New Hampshire.

In the **Republican presidential primaries**, Arizona Senator John McCain took the early lead by winning the New Hampshire primary, but from then on it was mostly wins for George W. Bush, son of former president George H.W. Bush.

At the Republican presidential nominating convention, Bush won easily. He named Texan Dick Cheney, the CEO of military contractor Halliburton Company as his running mate. Cheney had been Secretary of Defense under Bush's father, George H. W. Bush.

When somebody remembered that the Electoral College section of the U.S. Constitution states that the president and vice president cannot come from the same state, Cheney quickly got a driver's license from Wyoming and put his Texas home up for sale.

A third party candidate, **Ralph Nader**, nominee of the **Green Party**, was on the ballot in many states, and as it turned out, his presence on the ballot in Florida undoubtedly cost Gore the presidency.

The 2000 presidential campaign was mainly a battle of television ads, many of them negative (meaning they attacked the opponent rather than extolling the virtues of the candidate who placed the ad).

The three October debates were also important. In the first televised debate, those present in the auditorium felt Bush had performed very badly. In fact, right after the debate ended, Bush's handlers went on TV to attribute his poor showing to illness, saying he had not had adequate time to prepare for the debate. But when the polls came out the next day, a majority of the television viewing audience said they liked what they saw in George Bush. Many of those polled said he seemed like a "regular guy."

Gore accused Bush and the Republicans of being too "right wing" and too militaristic. There was also a lot of talk about where Bush's campaign funds were coming from.

Gore talked about the tax breaks **the wealthiest one percent** were getting, pointing out that it was **the other 99 percent** that were responsible for the country's current prosperity and the budget surplus, so why should the 99 percent have to pay more in taxes and the rich less.

The Bush campaign focused on the "Clinton-Gore" years in an attempt to tie Gore closely to the now-unpopular Bill Clinton.

Gore tried to distance himself from Clinton personally, but did often make reference to how Clinton had turned the budget deficits of the Republican years into a budget surplus.

Bush responded by saying Gore was using "fuzzy math."

The 2000 Election Outcome

Let's start our analysis of the 2000 election by looking first at the outcome. **Gore won the popular vote by 543,895 votes, but lost in the Electoral College by five votes.** Bush's margin of victory in the Electoral College should have been only four votes, but a faithless elector in Minnesota, a state that Gore won, **refused to cast his vote for Gore** and instead cast it for John Edwards.

The obvious question is, how could a candidate who won the popular vote by more than a half million votes lose in the Electoral College?

The answer goes all the way back to the **constitutional convention** in 1787 when, as a compromise with the slave states, the delegates agreed to give every state three Electoral College votes, no matter how small the state. Simply put, in the Electoral College, votes cast in states with small populations count for a lot more that votes in large population states. That reality was created as part of the Electoral College compromise more than two hundred years ago, and because it is in the U.S. Constitution, it is still true today. It would take a vote in Congress to change the Electoral College section of the Constitution, and then it would require ratification by three-fourths of the states. That is not likely to happen because the states with smaller populations would lose their advantage in selecting the president. Today, because the Republicans generally win the smaller states, they would undoubtedly block any attempt to get rid of the Electoral College system.

2000 presidential Election Results by Region.

Gore won the entire West Coast accounting for 7,829,197 of his popular vote total.

Gore also won **the East**, except for New Hampshire which he lost by only 7,211 votes.

In just three of the eastern states he won - New Jersey, New York, and Pennsylvania - he got 7,878,047 popular votes. As you can see, Gore racked up large pluralities in the states with the largest populations.

In **the Midwest**, Bush won the all-important Ohio vote with it's 21 Electoral College votes. However, Bush only won the popular vote by 165,019 (out of almost five million votes cast). In other words, in Ohio, Gore got **almost as many** votes as Bush, but got **zero Electoral College votes**.

In the **central Midwest, Gore won** Illinois, Iowa, Michigan, Minnesota, and Wisconsin which gave him 7,809,214 more popular votes.

It is important to note that in the states Gore won, **Nader was also strong**. Some say Gore would have won as many as a million more votes **if Nader had not been on the ballot** in those states, but that wouldn't have resulted in Gore wining **any more** electoral votes. Without Nader in the race in those states, **it is likely Gore would have won the popular vote by one and half million votes, but he still would not have been elected president.** (Those numbers will be important later when we analyze the potential popular votes for Obama in the upcoming 2012 election.)

Bush won western states with small populations, including Colorado, Idaho, Kansas, Montana, Nebraska, Nevada, North Dakota, Oklahoma, South Dakota, Utah, and Wyoming to accumulate **60**

Electoral College votes. The total number of voters in those states in 2000 was 9,394,171. In comparison, California had 10,965,856 voters, more than a million and a half more voters than the small western states, and yet **California only got 54 Electoral College votes**. It clearly illustrates the advantage the smaller-population states have in the Electoral College.

Bush won every southern state, but in some of those states **the vote was close**. The only southern states Bush won convincingly were Texas, his home state, and Alabama. In the other southern states, the vote was surprisingly close. In Tennessee, Bush won the popular vote by only 80,229 (out of more than two million votes cast). In Arkansas, he won by only 50,172 votes (out of almost a million votes cast). That meant Bush was picking up **all** the Electoral College votes in the South, but he wasn't gaining much advantage in the popular vote count.

In Florida, the outcome was extremely close, with Bush pulling out a very narrow win of 1,784 votes (out of 6 million votes cast).

However, the state-mandated recount found many irregularities. Somehow, a lot of votes for Gore had been missed. After the recount was finished, Bush's lead had been cut to only 537 votes. A second, more careful recount was ordered, and **the more votes that were recounted, the more Bush's lead dwindled**. When Bush's lead was down to only 154, Republicans went to court to put a stop to the recount. The Florida state Supreme Court said the recount was legal an should go on, but in an extremely controversial decisions, the U.S. Supreme Court, in a 5 to 4 vote, ordered the recount stopped permanently.

With the addition of Florida's 25 electoral votes, **Bush had 271 Electoral College votes, just one more than the required 270 needed to win the election**. Gore ended up with 266 electoral votes (one Gore elector from the District of Columbia left her ballot blank to protest their lack of representation in Congress). **Even though Al Gore had won the general election by more than half a million votes, he did not get to be president**.

It is interesting to note here that the framers of the Constitution intentionally left the members of the Electoral College free to vote for anyone they wanted to, possibly for just such a situation. A few

Republican electors could have realized it was unfair that the candidate who won the national vote was losing in the Electoral College and **they could have legally switched their votes to the winner of the popular vote**, Al Gore.

COMMENT:

The **Florida voting outcome in the 2000 presidential election** was very controversial, to say the least. With Bush's conservative Republican brother serving as the governor in Florida, most observers thought Bush would win the state's presidential election easily.

But Clinton had been a popular president there, and the state also had a large Hispanic and African-American population that traditionally voted Democratic. And although the fact that Gore's running mate, Joe Lieberman, was Jewish might have hurt the Democrats in the rest of the South, the large Jewish population in Florida ended up voting mostly for the Gore-Lieberman ticket.

The early pre-election polls showed the race was going to be closer in the state than people thought.

Soon after the polls closed, based on exit polling (the pollsters question voters as they leave the polling places), the national TV networks declared Gore the projected winner in Florida. Based on that result, they also projected Gore would win the Electoral College vote and therefore he would become the nation's forty-third president.

A significant moment in the election came after the TV networks had officially declared Gore their projected winner. Reporters asked if Bush was ready to concede Florida based on the exit poll results. Bush reminded them that his brother was the governor of Florida and went on to say we haven't given up yet, we are "working the phones." When the reporters asked what good "working the phones" would do now that the polls were already closed, there was no answer from either George Bush or his brother. Later that night, more results began to come in favoring Bush.

That kind of thing, along with the many voting irregularities that were being reported in Florida, made the Democrats suspicious. When voting results came in showing Bush had somehow overcome Gore's lead and had won by 1,784 votes, they got even more suspicious.

With a win that close (a Bush advantage of 1,784 votes out of 5,963,110 votes cast), Florida law required an automatic recount.

The closely scrutinized recount found Bush to have won by only 537 votes. The recount had somehow taken 1,247 votes away from Bush.

Based on the result of that first recount, the Democrats starting looking for other voting irregularities. They said in Escambia County, a predominately African-American district, 16% of the ballots were thrown out without explanation. In Columbia County, another predominately African-American district, 17% of the ballots were rejected. They analyzed the districts in which the largest numbers of ballots were thrown out and found out it was mostly happening in Democratic districts.

The Democrats began to analyze the 54,000 Florida citizens that had not been allowed to vote for one reason or another. Again, the majority of citizens that had not been allowed to vote turned out to be African-Americans. Further analysis discovered that many African-American voters had been turned away because their names had mistakenly been listed as felons.

One thing that drew special attention from the Democrats was a confusing type of paper ballot used in Palm Beach that became known as the "butterfly ballot." They said the Palm Beach voters were mostly Democrats who had been confused by the ballots which had made them mistakenly vote for Pat Buchanan of the Reform Party when they thought they were voting for Al Gore. Buchanan received 3,407 votes on the so-called butterfly ballots, and later, the chairman of the Palm Beach County's Reform Party said he believed there were only 400 to 500 Buchanan supporters in that Democratic stronghold. An analysis of the ballots showed most of those who had voted for Buchanan had otherwise voted Democratic. (Exit polls had previously indicated that most of the voters in that district said they had voted straight Democratic.) Later, Buchanan himself said, after looking at one of the so-called butterfly ballots, he could see how voters might have mistakenly voted for him when they thought they were voting for Al Gore.

For all these reasons, the Gore campaign requested that **disputed ballots in four counties be counted by hand,** Under Florida law, such a recount was allowable.

Although thousands of spoiled Bush-favoring absentee ballots from overseas soldiers **had been** recounted by hand to determine "the **voter's intent,**" the Bush campaign **fought hard against a manual recount of the rest of the votes. Katherine Harris**, the Republican Secretary of State in Florida stopped the recount. That prompted the Democrats to go to court to say that under Florida law, a manual recount should be allowed.

Harris argued against the recount in court until it was finally brought before **the Florida Supreme Court. They ordered the recount to be completed,** and it was resumed.

The problem for Bush was that the more ballots were recounted, the more votes he lost. After careful scrutiny of the first ballots, Bush's 1,784 vote lead soon shrank to only 154. **It was clear that if the recount was allowed to go on, Bush would lose**.

In desperation, the Republicans **asked the U.S. Supreme Court for an emergency decision to stop the recount**. They said Bush would suffer "irreparable harm" if the recount was allowed to continue.

The court's decision came quickly: **the Supreme Court voted five to four to permanently stop the recount**.

To this day, that decision is still one of the most controversial in the Supreme Court's history. The decision, and more importantly, the close 5-4 vote, is often used as an example when people talk about the president's power to "stack" the Supreme Court. Cynics would say you could have told in advance which of the judges were going to vote to stop the recount by simply noting which president appointed them.

The five judges who voted to stop the recount were:

Anthony Kennedy, appointed by Republican President Ronald Reagan.

Antonin Scalia, appointed by Republican President Ronald Reagan.

Sandra Day O'Connor, appointed by Republican President Ronald Reagan.

William Rehnquist, appointed by Republican President Richard Nixon.

Clarence Thomas, appointed by Republican President George H. W. Bush.

The four judges who voted against stopping the recount, Ruth Bader Ginsburg, Stephen Breyer, David Souter, and John Paul Stevens were quite vocal about their **opposition to the decision**. They denounced the decision as **a violation of both constitutional procedures and democratic principles**. They said the Florida Supreme Court was clearly within its legal and constitutional rights in allowing the recount to go forward, and therefore it was not appropriate for the U.S. Supreme Court to step in and override the highest court in the state of Florida. Justice Stevens pointed to historical legal precedent, saying, "On questions of state law, we have consistently respected the opinions of the highest courts of the states."

As for the strictly legal issues, the four dissenting judges said **the Republicans had failed to provide a legal basis** for the issuance of a stay. They said there was no evidence that Bush would suffer irreparable harm if the recount went on (other than he might lose the election). They asked how, in a democracy, carefully counting every vote could be a bad thing. They said the only danger of "irreparable harm" was to the public and to the democracy, and that going against Florida law to stop a recount would "cast a cloud on the legitimacy of the election."

Four of the five judges that had voted in favor of Bush's request to stop the Florida recount had nothing to say about why they had made that decision. Only Antonin Scalia commented, saying only that the decision had been made because there was no way to know if the ballots that were being counted were "legally cast." The four dissenting judges pointed out that there was nothing in the Bush request to stop the recount that said anything about "legally cast ballots." On the contrary, they said that was exactly the reason for the recount, to make sure every ballot counted had been legally cast. The five judges who had voted to stop the recount had no response to that. Nevertheless, even in a five-to-four decision, the Supreme Court is the final law of the land and the recount was stopped. **Katherine Harris** certified the election in favor of Bush and there was nothing Gore or the Democrats could do abut it.

Perhaps the most surprising outcome of the 2000 presidential election was the lack of outrage by the public over the fact that the winner of the popular votes did not get to be president.

Remember the 1824 election when Andrew Jackson had won the nation's popular vote, but didn't get to be president? Back then, the nation erupted in outrage. They said the people's wishes had been trampled on. Many demanded that the Electoral College decision be overturned and that Jackson be put into his rightful place as president.

When that didn't happen, Jackson demanded an end to the Electoral College system of electing the president. He said it was ridiculous that the people didn't get to vote for the most important office in the country. Nearly everyone agreed with him, and it was the closest the Electoral College system ever came to being thrown out. But of course, the states with smaller populations and the slave states were not about to give up their voting advantage in the Electoral College, so they fought against the effort to end it and were able to defeat the movement.

So what was different in 2000? Why did Gore, unlike Andrew Jackson, give up so easily?

In 1824, Jackson immediately said he would run again for president in the 1828 election. In the 1828 election, he used the unfairness of the 1824 election as the main reason why he should be elected president. As a result, he won the 1828 election in a landslide.

So why didn't Gore do the same thing that Jackson had done in 1824? Many think that if he had run again and kept on reminding people of what had happened in Florida and of the fact that he had actually won the 2000 general election by 543,895 votes, he would have won the 2004 presidential election easily. But that didn't happen. The reasons are complex and unfortunate, as we shall see.

Chapter Fifteen
Presidential Politics and the War on Terrorism

By the time the 2004 presidential election rolled around, Al Gore and the Electoral College debacle of 2000 was long forgotten because the nation was in an uproar over the events that had been put into motion on **September, 11, 2001**. On that date, 19 young men from Egypt, the United Arab Emirates, Lebanon, and Saudi Arabia commandeered four airliners in order to crash them into politically-important American buildings.

COMMENT:

The events of September 11, 2001 were put into play many months before when a few young Arab-looking men who spoke little English but had legal U.S. entry visas, asked about pilot training in San Diego. Through a translator, they said they wanted to learn to fly Boeing passenger jets, but they were told they would have to learn to fly small airplanes first. They said no, they were only interested in learning how to fly big passenger airliners. The flying instructors testified later that they thought the young men had big unrealistic dreams.

After the flying instruction began, the instructors said the students focused only on in-flight maneuvering and had little interest in learning about takeoffs and landings.

Later, other young men from Saudi Arabia entered the U.S. and began taking flying lessons in Florida where they eventually obtained commercial pilot's licenses. They never actually got the chance to fly any large planes, but in the spring of 2011, they were able to get training on a Boeing 737 simulator in Arizona.

That triggered interest from somebody who notified the Arizona FBI. The Arizona branch of the FBI alerted Washington headquarters that several Middle Easterners were training at a U.S. aviation school in Arizona, They recommended that other aviation schools nationwide be contacted to find out if other Arabs might be trying to learn how to fly large airplanes.

It is not known if anybody in the FBI, or in any other antiterrorist agency, took note of the warning. However, the FBI and other agencies must have been aware that airliner hijackings had long been a favorite way for militant groups to bring their causes to the public's attention. Over the previous forty years, there had been several instances where airliner hijackers reported that they were planning to crash their hijacked airliners into important buildings.

It is not known how far up the line the Arizona FBI report went, but it is now known that at least two of the hijackers were already on an FBI watch list.

After completing their pilot training in August of 2001, the hijackers bought tickets on four flights leaving from eastern cities with destinations in California. Planes leaving for cross-country flights were intentionally chosen to be sure they would have heavy loads of fuel on board.

Using box cutters as weapons and with the threat that bombs on board the plane, the five hijackers took control of American Airlines Flight 11 that had left Boston's Logan Airport at 7:59 AM. The hijackers flew that airliner into the North Tower of the World Trade Center at 8:46 AM.

Another airliner, American Airlines Flight 175, took off from Boston's Logan Airport at 8:14 AM. Five more hijackers took control of that airliner and flew it into the South Tower of the World Trade Center at 9:03 AM.

American Airlines Flight 77 took off from Washington's Dulles International Airport at 8:20 AM and another five hijackers took control of that plane and flew it into the Pentagon Building at 9:37 AM.

A forth airliner, United Airlines Flight 93 took off from Newark International Airport at 8:42 AM, and four more hijackers took control of that plane. Reportedly, several of the passengers tried to overcome the hijackers and the plane crashed into the ground near Shanksville, Pennsylvania at 10:03 AM.

Video of the two World Trade Center towers burning was soon being broadcast live on all the TV networks, and the nation watched in horror.

Unexpectedly, the south tower, the second tower to be hit, collapsed after burning for 56 minutes. Twenty one minutes later, the north tower also collapsed.

Later analysis determined that the collapse of both buildings was caused by the fire, not by the impact. The heat of burning jet fuel had melted important steel structural elements of the buildings. According to the 9/11 commission report, the buildings would not have collapsed if more fireproofing had been installed.

By the end of that dreadful day, 2,606 people had died in the two towers and 125 had died at the Pentagon. On the four airliners, 246 passengers and crew had died, along with the19 hijackers.

The attacks on 9/11 brought about many changes in the United States. In less than a month, U.S. military forces launched attacks in Afghanistan. It was the first stage of President Bush's new "war on terror." He said from now on, U.S. policy would be to go after terrorists and that the U.S. would not distinguish between terrorist organizations and nations or governments that harbored them.

Bush focused on one particular group of terrorists known as **al-Qaeda**, a widespread group of militants led by a Saudi citizen named **Osama bin Laden**. He was believed to be in Afghanistan, and it was believed he was in league with the Taliban, an Islamist militant group that controlled Afghanistan at that time.

As U.S. forces, with support from Britain and Australia, approached Kabul, the capital city of Afghanistan, the Taliban retreated. By the middle of November, the allied forces were in control of the country. (As of this writing, eleven years later, there are still 80,000 U.S. troops and an unknown number of military-support **"private contractors"** in Afghanistan.)

In the spring of 2003, President Bush's war on terror was expanded to Iraq. Alleging that **Iraq was harboring al-Qaeda** and that Iraqi President Saddam Hussein was in the process of developing **weapons of mass destruction,** President Bush sought approval from Congress to invade Iraq. Although Congress did not approve a formal declaration of war against Iraq, they did pass a joint resolution **authorizing military action** against Iraq. It was not an uncontested vote. In the House, the Republicans were nearly unanimously in favor of it, 215 to 6, but the Democrats votes against it, 126 to 82. The dissenters pointed out that United Nations inspectors had done a complete search of Iraq and had found **no evidence of any weapons of mass destruction** development and **no evidence of an al-Qaeda presence**. In fact, the United Nations experts said the brutal government of Iraq had been making sure there was no support for al-Qaeda in the country.

In the Senate, the Republicans, of course, supported their Republican president and voted in favor of military action, 48 to1. But what was surprising was that the majority of the Democratic senators also voted in favor, 29 to 21 against. It was not so surprising that essentially all of the senators from the conservative southern and middle western states voted in favor of military action in Iraq, but it was a surprise to many that some senators from the more liberal northern states also voted in favor of it. Senators like Kerry from Massachusetts, Clinton and Schumer from New York, Biden and Torricelli from New Jersey, Carper from Delaware, Feinstein from California, and Cantwell from Washington voted in favor of taking military action in Iraq.

However, by 2007, 28 of the 77 senators who had voted in favor of military action in Iraq said that if they knew then what they know now, they would have voted against the measure, meaning it would have failed in the senate, and Bush would not have had the authority to send U.S. troops to Iraq.

With congressional approval in hand, President Bush soon ordered air attacks on Iraq, and on March 20, 2003, the military invasion of Iraq began. With the support of extensive air power, the U.S. forces moved quickly, and within a few weeks, they took the capital city of Baghdad.

A month later, speaking from the deck of a U.S. aircraft carrier, USS Abraham Lincoln, President **Bush said the war in Iraq was over** and a new era in Iraq could begin.

In reality, it took more than eight more years and a new president before the last of the U.S. troops were withdrawn from Iraq.

All told, **well over a million members of the U.S. military** served in Iraq.

Despite the best medical care in any U.S. war, **4,484 American soldiers died** in Iraq, many of them from insurgent ambushes and from so-called **"improvised explosive devices"** (IEDs).

317 coalition forces from countries other than the U.S. also died in combat.

Estimates of the numbers of wounded American soldiers **vary widely from 100,000 to more than half a million**, depending on what type of injuries are counted.

The number of deaths and injuries to Iraqi civilians is unknown. **Civilian death estimates vary from 151,000 to over a million.** The number of injuries and deaths of Iraqi civilians **will probably never be known**.

At the end of 2011, President Obama withdrew the last of the U.S. troops from Iraq, but the war in Afghanistan goes on, making it the longest war in U.S. history.

The Presidential Election of 2004

The presidential election of 2004 was obviously going to be a referendum on the war in Iraq. Despite President Bush's pronouncement that the war was over in March of 2003, a year later, no weapons of mass destruction had been found and American soldiers were still dying over there.

There was also widespread criticism of Bush's conduct of the war, especially after accusations of torture, rape, and murder of military prisoners came out. Of special focus was the Abu Ghraib prison in

Iraq and the Guantanamo Bay detention camp in Cuba, both of which were managed by the U.S. military.

Nevertheless, no serious challengers appeared during the Republican primaries, and as a result, Bush was nominated by the Republican party to run for reelection. There were calls for him to dump his vice president, Dick Cheney, because he was such a strong advocate of what he referred to as "enhanced interrogation" of prisoners of war. Bush refused.

The Democratic primaries saw 10 candidates come forward. They were (in alphabetical order):

> Wesley Clark, retired U.S. Army general from Arkansas.
> Howard Dean, former governor of Vermont.
> John Edwards, U.S. Senator from North Carolina.
> Dick Gephardt, U.S. Representative from Missouri.
> Bob Graham, U.S. Senator from Florida.
> John Kerry, U.S. Senator from Massachusetts.
> Dennis Kucinich, U.S. Representative from Ohio.
> Joe Lieberman, U.S. Senator from Connecticut.
> Al Sharpton, civil rights activist from New York.
> Carol Moseley Braun, former senator from Illinois.

In the **Democratic primaries**, **Howard Dean** was the early favorite, but **John Kerry** pulled out a win in **New Hampshire**.

Then, in the **South Carolina** primary, **John Edwards** won.

In **Oklahoma**, **Wesley Clark** won, but Edwards was a close second.

But then, Kerry started to win some primaries. He won Hawaii, Idaho, Maine, Michigan, Nevada, Tennessee, Washington, and Washington, D.C. and then went on to win at the Democratic national nominating convention. He selected North Carolina Senator **John Edwards** as his running mate

The 2004 presidential campaign was, as predicted, mostly about Iraq and U.S. foreign policy. Kerry attacked Bush's handling of the war in Iraq, and he especially criticized the treatment of prisoners in Guantanamo Bay without regard to the Geneva Conventions, the body of international law that regulates the treatment of prisoners of war. Kerry said Bush had repeatedly acted without the support of the

United Nations, and his actions were hurting America's reputation abroad, even among America's allies.

Bush's campaign focused on the **worldwide terrorist threat**, and it seemed eerily similar to earlier Republican presidential campaigns during the Cold War that had focused on the **worldwide Communist threat**.

During the campaign, Bush defended his aggressive approach to fighting terrorism. One of his early campaign ads showed a picture of an Arab-looking man as it talked about the need to fight terrorism at home and abroad. His ads suggested Kerry would be weak on fighting terrorism. They suggested that in a crisis, Kerry would be slow to act.

The Kerry campaign responded by pointing out that he voluntarily served in Vietnam and had won service metals while Bush was "hiding out" in the Texas National Guard.

The Democrats said that Bush had used his father's political connections in Texas to get into easy Texas National Guard assignment. They said Bush rarely even bothered to perform his National Guard duties. They produced evidence that showed he was actually out of the state when National Guard records showed he was in attendance at National Guard meetings in Texas.

The Republicans tried to discredit the Texas National Guard documents, and they found some Vietnam veterans willing to say that Kerry's "dangerous" service in Vietnam was exaggerated, and that he didn't deserve the medals he had won. They pointed out that upon his return to the United States, Kerry had joined the veterans against the war in Vietnam movement, thus betraying his former comrades.

The Republicans also tried to discredit the reporters who had reported on Bush's missing service in the Texas National Guard.

In every instance, Bush defended his conduct of the "**war on terrorism**." His ads continued to focus on the Arab threat.

The implication was clear, if the voters liked his "preemptive" approach to fighting Arab terrorism in Afghanistan and Iraq, and if they felt the harsh treatment of Arabic prisoners was a fitting response to the Americans who had died on 9/11 and a way to get information that might help the U.S. military, then they should vote to reelect Bush and Cheney.

As it turned out, **Bush and Cheney won every southern state, and many of the midwestern and western states. Kerry won the West Coast, the upper Midwest, and the East.**

While **the popular vote was relatively close,** 50.73 percent to 48.27 percent in favor of Bush, the Electoral College vote was not as close - 286 for Bush and 251 for Kerry. Once again, the Republican dominance in the South and in the Western states with smaller populations had racked up enough Electoral College votes to win.

The Presidential Election of 2008

The **Presidential Election of 2008** was clearly going to be a referendum on how well Bush and the Republicans had handled the so-called war on terror. By the time the 2008 presidential election season began, national polls were indicating Bush would leave office as **one of the most unpopular presidents in U.S. history**. The polls showed he was even more unpopular than Richard Nixon after Nixon was forced to resign.

It was quite **a contrast to Bush's 90 percent approval rating** when he stood on the deck of the aircraft carrier USS Abraham Lincoln and declared "mission accomplished" in Iraq.

Paradoxically, when asked in 2008 why they disliked Bush's performance in office so much, most people mentioned the same thing that had formerly made him popular, the war in Iraq.

Vice President Dick Cheney's ratings were even lower than Bush's, with only thirteen percent of Americans saying they approved of his performance in office.

Nevertheless, **Bush and Cheney still had plenty of support among Republicans in the South**.

With the polls showing such strong disapproval of Bush, the Republicans undertook the uphill task of getting a Republican elected president in 2008.

Eleven candidates came forward to compete in the Republican primaries. They were (in alphabetical order):

Sam Brownback, U.s. Senator from Kansas.
Jim Gilmore, former Governor of Virginia.

Rudy Giuliani, former mayor of New York City.
Mike Huckabee, former Governor of Arkansas.
Duncan Hunter, U.S. Representative from California.
Alan Keyes, former ambassador from Maryland.
John McCain, U.S. Senator from Arizona.
Mitt Romney, former Governor of Massachusetts.
Tom Tancredo, U.S. Representative from Colorado.
Fred Thompson, former U.S. Senator from Tennessee.
Tommy Thompson, former Governor of Wisconsin.

The **Republican primaries** began, as usual with the Iowa caucuses. Mike Huckabee won, but then faded badly in New Hampshire. McCain won New Hampshire despite speculation that Rudy Giuliani or Mitt Romney would prevail.

After a third-place finish in Florida, Giuliani withdrew from the race and endorsed John McCain. From then on, **McCain** won most of the primaries, and he was nominated at the Republican national nominating convention in Minnesota. He surprised everyone by picking the outspoken conservative governor of Alaska, **Sarah Palin**, as his running mate.

With Bush's approval rating so low and the American public tired of hearing about the continuing deaths of American servicemen in Iraq and Afghanistan, the Democrats felt they had a good chance of taking back the White House in 2008.

Ten candidates came forward to compete in the Democratic primaries. They were (in alphabetical order):

Evan Bayh, U.S. Senator from Indiana.
Joe Biden, U.S. Senator from Delaware.
Hillary Clinton, U.S. Senator from New York.
Christopher Dodd, U.S. Senator from Connecticut.
John Edwards, former U.S. Senator from North Carolina.
Mike Gravel, former U.S. Senator from Alaska.
Dennis Kucinich, U.S. Representative from Ohio.
Barack Obama, U.S. Senator from Illinois.
Bill Richardson, Governor of New Mexico.
Tom Vilsack, former Governor of Iowa.

Many were surprised that Al Gore, the winner of the popular vote in 2000, wasn't among the candidates. At first he expressed interest, but eventually he decided against running again. The speculation was that he felt he was doing more good as an ambassador in **the fight against global warming**.

In the Iowa caucuses, the relatively unknown, but very eloquent, Barack Obama won, with John Edwards coming in second and Hillary Clinton third.

But Clinton made a comeback to win in New Hampshire.

There were January primaries in Michigan and Florida, both won by Clinton, but the Democratic National Committee disallowed them because they were held too early in the primary season. (Eventually, the Michigan and Florida votes were divided between Clinton and Obama.)

At the end of January, Obama won Nevada and South Carolina, but from that point on, Obama and Clinton alternated wins in the rest of the primaries.

The 2008 Democratic national presidential nominating convention was expected to be contentious with the delegates votes split between Obama and Clinton. Neither candidate had enough votes to win the nomination. However, midway through the voting, when it became clear that Obama was pulling into the lead, Clinton asked for Democratic unity and told her delegates to vote for Obama.

Barack Obama, the first-term senator from Illinois, was nominated by unanimous acclimation. He was the first person of African-American heritage to be nominated by a major party (his mother was white, but she had married Kenyan Barack Hussein Obama Sr. while he was in the U.S going to college).

Obama chose **Joe Biden**, a U.S. senator from Delaware, as his running mate.

The campaign focused on the two ongoing wars in Afghanistan and Iraq. Obama came out strongly against the Iraq war in particular, and McCain, who had supported the two wars all along, was forced to defend them.

Focusing on Bush's unpopularity, Obama reminded the voters that McCain had voted to support Bush 90 percent of the time.

McCain, as a long-time member of the U.S. Senate, focused on Obama's inexperience. He pointed out the fact that Obama was **a first-term senator**.

Obama countered that charge by saying it was time for a change. He pointed out how the Republicans had turned Clinton's healthy economy and budget surplus into an unhealthy economy and a rapidly-growing budget deficit. He said he would enact universal health care, make America "green," and bring back respect for America abroad.

COMMENT:

By the time voters went to the polls in 2008, the country was in the midst of a financial crisis. Only a few weeks before the 2008 election, Lehman Brothers, one of the world's largest financial institutions was forced to file for bankruptcy because of its exposure to newly-created risky and speculative financial instruments that were based on shaky subprime mortgages. Many other financial institutions around the world were also highly exposed to the new and very complicated financial instruments.

As the election neared, the situation was threatening to bring down America's entire financial system. Bush's Secretary of the Treasury, Henry Paulson, the former head of the Goldman Sachs investment banking company, had gone before Congress to ask for hundreds of billions to bail out the financial institutions. After much controversy, Congress finally authorized the money, and the crisis was averted for the time being. Nevertheless, investors in the stock market lost billions and the so-called "housing bubble" collapsed and many Americans found they owed much more on their homes than they were worth. With unemployment rising, many faced foreclosure.

As of this writing, with the 2012 presidential election season already underway, unemployment is still high and some parts of the economy are still struggling. The financial crisis of 2008 and the government's handling of it is sure to be one of the most important issues in the 2012 election campaign.

As election day neared in 2008, the polls were showing the economic crisis was by far the most important issue. Although Americans were aware of Obama's inexperience, that seemed to be less important than the fact that people were hurting economically and they wanted a change in Washington.

The election took place in an environment of financial anxiety and uncertainty. Although the Republicans again held most of the South, this time they lost Florida in a very close vote (McCain lost Florida by 236,148 votes out of eight million votes cast). McCain also lost Virginia in another close vote, and he lost North Carolina, but by only 14,177 votes (out of more than four million votes cast).

Obama won the East, some of the Midwest, and the West Coast. But McCain won 22 states, almost as many as Obama's 28. However, McCain's wins were all in states with smaller populations and fewer Electoral College votes. Obama won all the larger population states *and* enough of the South and Midwest to secure the Electoral College win and become the 44th president of the United States.

Chapter Sixteen
The Presidential Election of 2012

Now we come to this year's presidential election. It turned out to be one of the closest in U.S. history.

When primary season began, it was clear President Obama was going to run for reelection on the Democratic ticket, but the race for the Republican presidential nomination seemed wide open.

The Republican primaries began, as usual, with the caucuses in Iowa and primary balloting in New Hampshire. And as usual, a great deal of attention was paid to these first two primaries, but in the end, they did little to predict which candidate would win the Republican nomination.

The outcome of the January 3rd primary in Iowa was essentially a three-way tie between former Pennsylvania Senator Rick Santorum (24.56%), former Massachusetts governor Mitt Romney (24.53%), and Texas Representative Ron Paul (21.43%).

The New Hampshire primaries were held a week later. As an indication of how wide open the Republican race was, 33 candidates filed to appear on the ballot. A televised debate was held a few days before the primary elections between former House speaker Newt Gingrich, former Utah governor Jon Huntsman, Texas Representative Ron Paul, Texas Governor Rick Perry, former Massachusetts governor Mitt Romney, and former Pennsylvania senator Rick Santorum

Mitt Romney campaigned heavily in New Hampshire, and the results indicated he was, for the moment at least, the front runner. He won the primary balloting with 39% of the vote, with Ron Paul coming in a distant second with 23% of the vote. Jon Huntsman, Rick Santorum, Newt Gingrich, and Rick Perry followed, but with much lower percentages of the vote.

The next primary, in South Carolina, was expected to clarify the situation, but it did the opposite. Newt Gingrich won, getting more than 40% of the total vote. Mitt Romney came in second, but with only 28% of the vote, followed by Rick Santorum, Ron Paul, and newcomer to the race, Herman Cain.

It looked like Romney's chances were diminishing. If he could not win the South, it would be unlikely that he would win the nomination.

The all-important state of Florida was next. Many saw it as a must-win for Romney, and he campaigned heavily there. Romney won with 46% of the vote, followed by Newt Gingrich, Rick Santorum, and Ron Paul.

COMMENT:

The primary elections of 2012 were the first presidential primary elections to be held after a landmark Supreme Court five-to-four decision that had lifted the restrictions on corporate contributions to political campaigns. As expected, the amounts spent on the candidates' campaigns broke all the prior spending records.

Rick Santorum managed to win a few more states before Super Tuesday, March 6th, the day ten states were to hold their primaries.

In the Super Tuesday primaries, Romney carried six states and Santorum three. Gingrich won his home state of Georgia. Romney was in the lead, but it was not a decisive lead.

Over the next few weeks, twelve more primaries were held, with Romney winning most of them. Baring any unforeseen surprises, it was beginning to look like Romney would be the nominee.

While the Republican primaries were going on, President Obama's approval rating was gradually going down. The early polls that posited a Romney-Obama presidential race showed Romney with surprising strength, given that he was up against a sitting president who had been elected by a large margin in 2008.

In the spring of 2012, looking at those polls, I began to wonder if some of the states that had voted for Obama in 2008 would revert to their **traditionally Republican voting patterns** and go for Romney. I looked at recent local elections in those states and discovered that they had mostly been electing Republican governors and senators. It looked like the presidential race in 2012 was going to be close, and that brought up the possibility that what had happened in the 2000 presidential election, a split popular/electoral vote, could happen again this time.

In the first week of April, I began writing a book about the history of our presidential elections and the role the Electoral College has played. I gave it the speculative title, *Obama Will Win, but Romney Will Be President.*

Because of the winner-take-all design of the Electoral College (in all states except Maine and Nebraska), it was clear that the presidential election of 2012 would come down to a few "swing states," states that did not consistently vote for either the Democratic candidate or the Republican candidate. In that book, I listed a handful of states that would probably end up deciding who our next president would be. I analyzed their voting history and their recent voting patterns. Based on that analysis, it seemed very likely that President Obama would win the popular vote because he would build up a large vote margin in many of the states that had the largest populations. However, because **the Electoral College has a built-in bias** that favors the small states, it was not at all clear that he could win the electoral vote.

That book was published early in May. From that moment on, I kept a close eye on the presidential polls and posted them on my Facebook author site, along with other important developments in the 2012 presidential campaign:

www.facebook.com/EverettEMurdockPhd

Early on, pre-nomination polls consistently showed President Obama in the lead, but **the margin was never all that great,** and there were always enough undecided voters to change the outcome.

As expected, the Republicans nominated Mitt Romney, and the Democrats nominated Barack Obama.

At the time, it seemed likely that **the two biggest campaign issues would be foreign policy and the domestic economy.** President Obama had withdrawn most of the U.S. troops from Iraq after the long war there, but the situation was still unstable. What would happen to that country without a U.S. military presence was an open question. And then there was the issue of the ongoing war in Afghanistan, the longest war in U.S. history. The Republicans revealed statistics that indicated Obama's war policies in Afghanistan were failing. They said Afghanistan was a more dangerous place now than it was when he took office. During the 2008 campaign, Obama had been critical of President Bush's handling of the war in Afghanistan, but after taking office, he had retained President Bush's Secretary of Defense, Robert Gates, and had approved the same "surge" approach (increasing the number of troops and fighting resources) Bush had used in Iraq and Nixon had used in Vietnam.

No one really knew what Romney's position would be in Afghanistan. He would need to appear to be tough on terrorism, but was the country ready for another escalation of the conflict in Afghanistan? President Obama had promised to get U.S. troops out by 2014 and turn the defense of the country over to the Afghans. That was the approach he had used in Iraq, but it was still an open question as to whether it was going to work. There had been a sustained increase in violence in Iraq after the U.S. troops were pulled out. Some people worried that Iraq would go the way of Vietnam.

In the two presidential elections since the 9-11 attack on the twin trade towers of the World Trade Center in New York City, both presidential candidates had said they would be tough on terrorism. But after two prolonged wars, would the American people be as keen on foreign wars of invasion? Because neither candidate would want to be blamed for a Vietnam-like debacle, it seemed possible that the ongoing war in Afghanistan **would not** be as big an issue as many were predicting. In fact, they both might agree that it was time to get our troops out.

Another issue sure to be of concern in the election was the so-called "Arab spring" uprisings. When the people of several Middle Eastern countries rose up to oust their despotic rulers, the Obama administration had been generally supportive. Obama had supported the rebels in Egypt and Libya, and as the 2012 presidential campaign got underway, it was still an open question as to whether the groups that took power as a result of those uprisings would be entirely friendly to the U.S.

In the past, Republican presidential candidates had tried to paint the Democrats as weak on defense. Republican candidates generally supported a strong military and showed more of a willingness to get involved in foreign civil wars than the Democratic candidates. After the 9-11 attacks on the twin towers in New York City, President Bush had not only approved the military invasions of Iraq and Afghanistan, but had also instigated a **"war on terror"** at home and abroad. He had created a huge new division of government, the Department of Homeland Security, and had instituted new policies that many said were an attack on the privacy and freedoms of all Americans. Obama had kept all of those policies in place, and had ordered the CIA and Navy SEALs operation that went into Pakistan and **killed Osama bin Laden**, the one-time leader of the al-Qaeda terrorist organization. Obama was sure to bring that fact up as often as possible. How would Romney respond?

The issue of **the country's ongoing economic problems was sure to be a major campaign issue**. A sitting president must always run on his record, and from the outset, it was clear Mitt Romney would campaign against President Obama's handling of the economy. The unemployment rate had stayed stubbornly high throughout Obama's four-year term. Obama had constantly pointed out that it was the previous Republican administration that had handed him an economy that was near collapse, and he had done his best to stabilize the situation through bailouts and government economic stimulus programs. He said the economy was recovering as well as could be expected, given how bad it had been.

Romney told the voters that as an experienced businessman he could do a better job of getting the U.S. economy back on its feet. That raised questions as to where he stood with regard to those in the financial industries who were widely seen as causing the country's severe economic downturn. President Obama tried to portray him as one of them.

Even the people who supported President Obama were not sure he had done enough to rein in the perpetrators of the near economic collapse. Many of the leaders of the nation's largest financial institutions were still in power and no one had been sent to jail. Obama had kept many of President Bush's top regulators in power, but he said he had to maintain the existing system to prevent an economic recession from spinning down into a depression.

Romney said the bailouts and the economic stimulus packages were the wrong approach. He laid out a five-point plan that had the blessing of many top economists. But more importantly, he asked the voters to look at their own lives and ask themselves if they were better off after four years of an Obama presidency. Many believed the outcome of the 2012 election would be determined by how people answered that question.

One thing was clear: in the spring of 2012, the polls were already indicating that the race would be very close; Obama would not coast to the kind of easy victory he had enjoyed in 2008.

At that time, I undertook a state-by-state analysis of each state's voting patterns to determine the likely outcome of the 2012 Electoral College vote. I categorized each state as likely to vote Republican, likely to vote Democrat, or as a "**swing state**" (a state that could swing either way). Below is a recap of that analysis.

Alabama - 9 Electoral Votes

Alabama had voted for the Republican candidate in the previous eight presidential elections.

Alabama's current governor was a Republican as were both of its senators.

Romney was leading in all the polls in Alabama. Therefore, it seemed very likely that Romney would win Alabama, which would give him 9 electoral votes.

Alaska - 3 Electoral Votes

Alaska had voted for the Republican candidate in the previous eleven presidential elections.

Alaska's current governor was a Republican and one of its senators was a Republican.

In the spring of 2012, it seemed very likely that Romney would win Alaska. Along with Alabama's 9 electoral votes, that would give Romney 12 electoral votes.

Arizona - 11 Electoral Votes

Except for 1996, when southern Governor Bill Clinton squeaked out a 31,215 vote win (Ross Perot got 112,072 votes), Arizona had voted for the Republican candidate in the last nine presidential elections.

Arizona's current governor was a Republican as were both of its senators.

In the spring of 2012, Romney was leading in all the polls in Arizona, and it seemed very likely that he would win that state, giving him a total of 23 electoral votes.

Arkansas - 6 Electoral Votes

Since 1976, Arkansas had voted for the Republican presidential candidate, except in 1992 and 1996 when they voted for favorite son, Democrat Bill Clinton.

Arkansas's newest senator was a Republican.

In the spring of 2012, Romney was leading in all the polls in Arkansas, and it seemed very likely that he would win that state, giving him 29 electoral votes.

California - 55 Electoral Votes

California had voted for the Democratic candidate in the previous five presidential elections.

California's current governor was a Democrat as were both of its senators.

In the spring of 2012, Obama was leading in all the polls in California, and it seemed very likely that he would win that state. With California's 55 electoral votes, Obama would take the lead 55 to 29.

Colorado - 9 Electoral Votes

Colorado had a long history of voting for the Republican candidate in presidential elections. However, Clinton won in 1992 (but not in 1996), and in 2008 the state went to Obama.

Colorado's recent governor and senate races had been hard fought wins for the Democrats. However, in the spring of 2012, the presidential polls in Colorado were showing a tight race with Obama holding a narrow lead over Romney.

It seemed very likely that Colorado would be one of the swing states that would decide the election. Putting Colorado aside for the moment would leave Obama with a lead of 55 to 29.

Connecticut - 7 Electoral Votes

Connecticut had voted for the Democratic candidate in the previous five presidential elections.

Connecticut's current governor was a Democrat as were both of its senators.

In the spring of 2012, Obama was leading in all the polls in Connecticut, and it seemed very likely that he would win that state, and that would give him a lead of 62 to 29.

Delaware - 3 Electoral Votes

Delaware had voted for the Democratic candidate in the previous five presidential elections.

Delaware's current governor was a Democrat as were both of its senators.

In the spring of 2012, it seemed very likely that Obama would win Delaware, which would give him a lead of 65 to 29.

Florida - 29 Electoral Votes

The disputed outcome of the voting in Florida in 2000 put considerable focus on that state in the 2012 election. Would the voting be as close as it had been in 2000? Florida had a long history of voting for Republican presidential candidates; however, in 1996, they voted for Southerner Bill Clinton, and in 2000, as we have seen, the Democratic candidate Al Gore got *at least* half the votes in the state.

In the spring of 2012, Obama was leading in the polls, but his lead was only a few percentage points, and the citizens of Florida had recently elected a conservative Republican governor and a conservative Republican senator.

As in 2000, it seemed likely that Florida would end up being one of the most important swing states. Putting aside Florida for the moment would leave Obama with a lead of 65 to 29 electoral votes.

Georgia - 16 Electoral Votes

Except for 1992, when Democratic Bill Clinton, a Southerner, squeaked out a close win, Georgia had voted for the Republican candidate in the prior seven presidential elections.

Georgia's current governor was a Republican as were both of its senators.

In the spring of 2012, Romney was leading in all the polls in Georgia, and it seemed very likely that he would win that state, making it a somewhat closer race, but with Obama still ahead 65 to 45.

Hawaii - 4 Electoral Votes

The island state of Hawaii had voted for the Democratic candidate in the previous six presidential elections.

Hawaii's current governor was a Democrat. The state had one Republican senator and one Democratic senator.

In the spring of 2012, Obama was leading in all the polls in Hawaii, and it seemed very likely that he would win his birth state of Hawaii, and that would give him a lead of 69 to 45.

Idaho - 4 Electoral Votes

Idaho had voted for the Republican candidate in the previous ten presidential elections.

Idaho's current governor was a Republican as were both of its senators.

In the spring of 2012, it seemed very likely that Romney would win Idaho, but Obama would still be ahead 69 to 49.

Illinois - 20 Electoral Votes

Illinois, President Obama's home state, is a populous state with a lot of electoral votes. In the prior five presidential elections, the state had gone to the Democratic candidate; however, in the five presidential elections before 1992, the state had gone to the Republican candidate. When Democrat Carter won the presidency in 1976, Illinois went for Republican Gerald Ford, so it was not easy to say which way the state would go in 2012.

The trick to figuring out who would win Illinois in 2012 was to analyze the state's voting history county by county. As of the last census, Cook County (Chicago and environs) had a population of 5,200,950. The entire rest of the state had only 7,668,307 people combined. Chicago almost always votes for the Democratic candidate; therefore, the question was, could the Republican candidate get enough votes in the rest of the state to overcome the likely Cook County Democratic lead? In the last close presidential election, in 2000, over 20 downstate counties - in addition to Cook County - went for Democratic candidate Al Gore, thus assuring Gore a close victory in Illinois. If Obama could also win those 20+ downstate counties in 2012, it would determine which way Illinois went.

In the spring of 2012, the polls in Illinois were mixed. Some said Romney was in the lead, others said Obama was ahead.

The state had a Democratic governor, but it had recently elected a Republican senator. Nevertheless, it seemed likely that Chicago's powerful Democratic political machine would be able to deliver Chicago for Obama. If the downstate counties voted the way they did in 2000, Obama would win Illinois. That would give him a substantial Electoral College lead of 89 to 49.

Indiana - 11 Electoral Votes

Indiana was another state that was hard to figure out. In 2008, Obama squeaked out a very close win there, winning by only 28,391 votes out of a total vote of 2,756,340. But in the nine presidential elections before that, the state had always gone for the Republican presidential candidate.

Indiana's current governor was a Republican as were both of its senators.

In the spring of 2012, Romney was leading in all the polls in Indiana. It seemed likely that Romney would win Indiana, but it might be close. If Romney did win Indiana, it would still leave Obama with an Electoral College lead of 89 to 60.

Iowa - 6 Electoral Votes

Iowa was another state that was hard to call. In 1948, the state went for Democrat Truman in a close election that mirrored the indecision seen throughout the country that year. After that, Iowa generally voted Republican. But then Democrat Johnson won in 1964. After 1964, Iowa went back to voting for the Republican presidential candidate until 1988, when they occasionally started voting for the Democratic presidential candidate. In 2000, they voted against Bush, but voted for him in 2004. In 2008, they reversed course again and went for Obama. So which way would they go in 2012? It was hard to say, but one thing was certain, it would be close.

The state had recently elected a Republican governor. It had one Republican senator, and one Democratic senator, but that didn't provide me with much up-to-date information about the sentiment of the voters because both senators had been in office for a long time.

As for the polls, in the spring of 2012, most showed Obama ahead, with Romney closing. However, the Des Moines Register, one of Iowa's most read newspapers, did a poll that found Romney in the lead. It seemed clear that Iowa would be one of the swing states to decide the 2012 presidential election. Putting aside Iowa for now would still leave Obama with an Electoral College lead of 89 to 60.

Kansas - 6 Electoral Votes

Kansas had voted for the Republican candidate in the previous eleven presidential elections.

Kansas's current governor was a Republican as were both of its senators.

In the spring of 2012, Romney was leading in all the polls in Kansas. Therefore, it seemed likely that he would win Kansas. That would keep Obama in the lead, 89 to 66.

Kentucky - 8 Electoral Votes

Kentucky had voted for the Republican candidate in every presidential election except when they voted for Democrat Southerners Clinton and Carter.

Kentucky had elected a Democratic governor back in 2007, but both of its senators were Republicans.

Romney was leading in all the polls in Kentucky.

It seemed likely that Romney would win Kentucky, and that would give him 74 electoral votes, still somewhat behind Obama's 89.

Louisiana - 8 Electoral Votes

Louisiana had voted for the Republican candidate in every presidential election, except when they voted for Democratic Southerners Clinton and Carter.

Louisiana had recently elected a conservative Republican governor and a Republican senator.

Romney was leading in all the polls in Louisiana. Therefore, in the spring of 2012, it seemed likely that he would win Louisiana, giving him 82 electoral votes which would bring him closer to Obama's total of 89.

Maine - 4 Electoral Votes

Maine had voted for the Democratic candidate in the last five presidential elections and there was no reason to think the 2012 election would be any different.

However, Maine had recently broken that tradition by electing a Republican governor, and it had two long-term women Republican senators. However, in the spring of 2012, Obama was leading in all the polls in Maine.

Maine is one of only two states (with Nebraska) that does not use the winner-take-all method of assigning electoral votes. It seemed likely that Obama would win Maine, but Romney might pick up one electoral vote there. That would give Obama 92 electoral votes as compared with Romney's 83.

Maryland - 10 Electoral Votes

Maryland had voted for the Democratic candidate in the past five presidential elections.

Maryland had a Democratic governor and both its senators were Democratic.

In addition, Obama was leading in all the polls in Maryland.

In the spring of 2012, it seemed likely Obama would win Maryland. That would give him 102 electoral votes as compared with Romney's 83.

Massachusetts - 11 Electoral Votes

Massachusetts has voted for the Democratic candidate in the past six presidential elections. Although Romney, the former governor of the state, still has some support there, it seemed likely that the state would continue to vote for Democratic candidates.

Massachusetts had a Democratic governor, but after long-time Senator Ted Kennedy died, his seat had been filled by a relatively unknown Republican. Nevertheless, in the spring of 2012, Obama was leading in all the polls in Massachusetts, and it seemed likely that he would win the state. That would bring his electoral total to 113 as compared to Romney's 83.

Michigan - 16 Electoral Votes

Michigan voted for the Democratic candidate in the past five presidential elections. Mitt Romney grew up in Michigan where his father was governor.

Michigan had a Republican governor, but it also had two Democratic senators.

Michigan had been hit hard by the slowdown in the economy and a lot of auto production had been moved out of the country. Nevertheless, with Democratic support, the government bailouts of the American auto industry had helped many auto-related businesses in Michigan making it more likely the state's voters would continue to support Democratic candidates. In the spring of 2012, it seemed likely that Obama would win Michigan as he had in 2008, but it also seemed likely that the presidential race in that state would be close. If Obama was able to hold onto Michigan, it would bring his electoral total to 129 as compared to Romney's 83.

Minnesota - 10 Electoral Votes

Minnesota had voted for the Democratic candidate in the last nine presidential elections.

Minnesota had a Democratic governor and two Democratic senators, and Obama was leading in the polls. Therefore, in the spring of 2012, it seemed likely that he would hold onto Minnesota, bringing his electoral total to 139 compared to Romney's 83.

Mississippi - 6 Electoral Votes

Mississippi had voted for the Republican candidate in each of the last eight presidential elections.

Mississippi's current governor was a Republican as were both of its senators.

Romney was leading in all the polls in Mississippi. Therefore, it seemed likely that he would win Mississippi. That would bring his total to 89 as compared to Obama's 139.

Missouri - 10 Electoral Votes

Missouri had voted for the Republican candidate in the last three presidential elections. They voted against Obama in 2008, but in the spring of 2012, the polls in Missouri were mixed.

Missouri had a Democratic governor, but they had recently elected a Republican senator.

In the spring of 2012, it seemed to me that Romney was likely to win Missouri, but not by all that much. If he did win, it would bring his electoral total up to 99 as compared to Obama's 139.

Montana - 3 Electoral Votes

Montana had voted for the Republican candidate in nine out of the past ten presidential elections (Clinton squeaked out a win over Bush in 1992 after Ross Perot got nearly as many votes as either of them).

Montana currently had a Democratic governor and both of it senators were Democrats, but Romney had a big lead in all the polls.

It seemed likely that Romney would win Montana, bringing his electoral total up to 102 as compared to Obama's 139.

Nebraska - 5 Electoral Votes

Nebraska had voted for the Republican candidate in the last eleven presidential elections.

Nebraska had a Republican governor, a Republican senator, and a Democratic senator.

Nebraska is one of only two states (with Maine) that does not use the winner-take-all method of assigning electoral votes. In the 2008 election, McCain won the state, but Obama received enough popular votes to pick up one electoral vote.

In the spring of 2012, the polls showed Romney with a big lead in Nebraska, and it seemed likely that he would win all of Nebraska's electoral votes. That would bring his total up to 107 as compared to Obama's 139.

Nevada - 6 Electoral Votes

Nevada had a mixed pattern of voting. They voted for Obama in 2008, but they voted for Bush in the two prior elections. They voted for Democrat Clinton in 1992 and 1996, but they voted for the Republican candidate in the five presidential elections before that.

Nevada had recently elected a Republican governor and a Republican senator.

In the spring of 2012, Obama was leading in the polls in Nevada, but it was close. Nevada seemed likely to be one of the key swing states that would decide the presidential election. Putting aside Nevada for time being, Obama would still have the Electoral College lead, 139 to Romney's 107.

New Hampshire - 4 Electoral Votes

New Hampshire had a history of being a swing state. However, it went for Obama in 2008, and so far, Obama was leading in all the New Hampshire polls.

New Hampshire had a Democratic governor, but the state had recently elected a Republican senator.

In the spring of 2012, it seemed likely that Obama would win New Hampshire, but New Hampshire had surprised us before. It seemed possible that New Hampshire would turn out to be one of the key swing states that would decide the election. Putting aside New Hampshire for now, Obama would still have the Electoral College lead, 139 to Romney's 107.

New Jersey - 14 Electoral Votes

New Jersey had voted for the Democratic candidate in the last five presidential elections.

Both of the state's current senators were Democrats, but the state had recently elected a Republican governor.

Nevertheless, in the spring of 2012, Obama was leading in all the New Jersey polls, and it seemed likely that he would win the state. That would bring Obama's total up to 153 compared to Romney's 107.

New Mexico - 5 Electoral Votes

New Mexico went for Obama in 2008, but the state went for Republican Bush in 2004 in an extremely close race (Bush won by only 5,988 votes). In 2000, Democrat Gore won New Mexico by only 366 votes (out of 598,605 votes cast).

Both of New Mexico's senators were Democrats, but the state had recently elected a Republican Hispanic woman governor.

Obama was leading in the polls, but not by all that much.

46% of New Mexico's citizens are Hispanic. If either candidate wanted to win New Mexico, they would have to win the Hispanic vote, but given the Republican party's hard line against illegal immigration, that would be tough.

In the spring of 2012, Obama had a big lead in New Mexico making it likely he would win the state. That would bring his total up to 158 as compared to Romney's 107.

New York - 29 Electoral Votes

New York had voted for the Democratic candidate in the last six presidential elections.

New York currently had a Democratic governor and both of its senators were Democrats.

In addition, Obama was leading in all the polls there, making it very likely that he would win New York in 2012. That would bring his total up to 187 as compared to Romney's 107.

North Carolina - 15 Electoral Votes

In 2008, Obama beat McCain in North Carolina, but only by 14,177 votes (out of 4,310,789 votes cast). In the seven presidential elections before 2008, North Carolina voted for the Republican candidate.

North Carolina currently had a Republican governor, a Republican senator, and a Democratic senator.

However, in the spring of 2012, the polls all showed Romney in the lead. Therefore, although I expected the outcome to be close, it seemed likely that North Carolina would revert back to its normal voting pattern and go for the Republican, Mitt Romney. That would bring Romney's electoral total up to 122 as compared to Obama's 187.

North Dakota - 3 Electoral Votes

North Dakota had voted for the Republican candidate in the last eleven presidential elections.

North Dakota's governor was a Republican and they had recently elected a Republican senator. In addition, Romney was leading in all the polls in North Dakota. Therefore, it seemed likely that he would win North Dakota, bringing his total up to 125 as compared to Obama's 187.

Ohio - 18 Electoral Votes

Ohio voted for Obama in 2008, but it was close. Prior to that, the state usually went for the Republican candidate. The state had gone for Republican George W. Bush in the two prior elections, but back in 1992, Democrat Clinton, a southern governor, had squeaked out a narrow win over George H. W. Bush after Ross Perot took more than a million votes.

Ohio had recently elected a Republican governor and a Republican senator.

It is worth noting that no Republican has ever won the presidency without winning Ohio.

In the spring of 2012, Obama was leading in the polls in Ohio. However, based on the state's history of voting for Republicans, it seemed likely that in 2012, Ohio would be one of the key swing states that would decide the election. In fact, it was possible that Ohio would be *the* state that decided the presidency. Putting Ohio aside for the time being would leave Obama in the lead 187 to Romney's 125.

Oklahoma - 7 Electoral Votes

Oklahoma had voted for the Republican candidate in the last eleven presidential elections.

Oklahoma's current governor was a Republican as were both of its senators. It seemed very likely that Romney would win Oklahoma, bringing his total up to 132 as compared to Obama's 187.

Oregon - 7 Electoral Votes

Oregon had voted for the Democratic candidate in the past six presidential elections.

Oregon's current governor was a Democrat as were both of its senators.

In the spring of 2012, Obama was leading in all the polls in Oregon. As a result, it seemed very likely he would win Oregon, bringing his total up to 194 as compared to Romney's 132.

Pennsylvania - 20 Electoral Votes

Pennsylvania had voted for the Democratic candidate in the previous five presidential elections.

Pennsylvania had a long-term Democratic senator, but the state had recently elected a Republican governor and a Republican senator. Nevertheless, in the spring of 2012, Obama was leading in all the polls in Pennsylvania. Therefore, given the state's history and the recent polls, it seemed likely that Obama would win Pennsylvania, but it would probably be a very close election. That would bring Obama's electoral total up to 214 as compared to Romney's 132.

Rhode Island - 4 Electoral Votes

Rhode Island had voted for the Democratic candidate in the last six presidential elections.

Rhode Island's current governor was elected as a liberal independent, and both of its senators were Democrats. In the spring of 2012, the Rhode Island polls were showing Obama to be in the lead. Therefore, it seemed likely that he would win Rhode Island, bringing his total up to 218 as compared to Romney's 132.

South Carolina - 9 Electoral Votes

South Carolina had voted for the Republican candidate in the previous eight presidential elections.

South Carolina's current governor was a Republican as were both of its senators.

Romney was leading in all the polls in South Carolina making it very likely that he would win the state. That would bring his total up to 141 as compared to Obama's 218.

South Dakota - 3 Electoral Votes

South Dakota had voted for the Republican candidate in the previous eleven presidential elections.

South Dakota had a Republican senator and a long-term Democratic senator. However, the state had recently elected a Republican governor and Romney was leading in the polls there. It seemed likely Romney would win South Dakota, bringing his total up to 144 as compared to Obama's 218.

Tennessee - 11 Electoral Votes

Except for 1992 and 1996, when the state went for Democrat Southerner Bill Clinton, Tennessee had voted for the Republican candidate in every presidential election since Southerner Jimmy Carter won in 1976.

Tennessee's current governor was a Republican as were both of its senators.

In the spring of 2012, Romney was leading in the polls, and it seemed very likely that Romney would win Tennessee. That would bring his total up to 155 as compared to Obama's 218.

Texas - 38 Electoral Votes

Texas had voted for the Republican candidate in the previous eight presidential elections.

Texas's current governor was a Republican as were both of its senators.

Romney was leading in all the polls in Texas indicating he was very likely to win the state. That would bring his total up to 193 as compared to Obama's 218.

Utah - 6 Electoral Votes

Utah had voted for the Republican candidate in the previous eleven presidential elections.

Utah's current governor was a Republican as were both of its senators.

It seemed very likely that Mormon Romney would win Utah, the predominately Mormon state. That would bring his total up to 199, somewhat closer to Obama's 218.

Vermont - 3 Electoral Votes

Vermont had voted for the Democratic candidate in the past five presidential elections.

Vermont's current governor was a Democrat as were both of its senators. In addition, Obama was leading in all the polls there making it very likely that he would win the state. That would bring his total up to 221 as compared to Romney's 199.

Virginia - 13 Electoral Votes

In 2008, Obama won the Virginia presidential election in a very close race. However, Virginia had voted for the Republican candidate in the prior ten presidential elections.

Virginia currently had a Republican governor and two long-term Democratic senators.

In the spring of 2012, Romney was leading in the polls in Virginia, but it was close. At that time, it seemed as though Virginia could be one of the key swing states that would decide the presidential election. Putting aside Virginia would leave Obama with a lead of 221 as compared to Romney's 199.

Washington - 12 Electoral Votes

Washington had voted for the Democratic candidate in the past six presidential elections.

Washington's current governor was a Democrat as were both of its senators. In addition, Obama was leading in all the polls. It seemed very likely that he would win the state of Washington. That would bring his electoral total up to 233 as compared to Romney's 199.

Washington D. C. - 3 Electoral Votes

It required an amendment to the United States Constitution (the Twenty-Third Amendment) in 1961 to give the citizens of the District of Columbia any say in who would be president and vice president (they are still not allowed to vote for representatives or senators). The amendment restricts Washington D.C. to three electoral votes, no matter how many people live there.

The first presidential election in which they got to vote for president and vice president was in 1964. They voted for the Democratic candidate, Lyndon Johnson, and have voted for the Democratic candidate in every presidential election since.

It seemed certain that Obama would win Washington D.C. That would bring his total up to 236 as compared to Romney's 199.

West Virginia - 5 Electoral Votes

West Virginia had voted for the Republican presidential candidate in the last three elections.

West Virginia currently had a Democratic governor and two Democratic senators, however in the spring of 2012, the polls showed a big lead for Romney.

In 1992 and 1996, West Virginia went for Democrat Southerner Bill Clinton. In 1998, the state went for Republican George H. W. Bush over Democrat Dukakis in a very close vote (Bush won by only 30,951 votes). The state gave McCain a strong majority over Obama in 2008. It seemed likely the state would go for Republican Romney in 2012. That would bring Romney's total up to 204 as compared to Obama's 236.

Wisconsin -10 Electoral Votes

Wisconsin had voted for the Democratic candidate in the past six presidential elections, but before that they often voted for the Republican candidate.

Wisconsin had recently elected a conservative Republican governor and a Republican senator.

Wisconsin polls showed Obama ahead, although not by all that much. It seemed evident that Wisconsin could be one of the swing states that would decide the 2012 presidential election.

Putting aside Wisconsin for now would leave Obama with a lead of 236 over Romney's 204.

Wyoming - 3 Electoral Votes

Wyoming had voted for the Republican candidate in the last eleven presidential elections.

Wyoming's current governor was a Republican as were both of its senators.

In the spring of 2012, it seemed very likely that Romney would win Wyoming, bringing his total up to 207 as compared with Obama's 236.

What It All Adds up To

When I looked only at the states where the outcome seemed assured, I found 24 states that were likely to be in the Romney camp, and 19 states that were likely to be in the Obama camp. However, more of the states that were likely to vote for Obama were states with larger populations which meant they had more electoral votes. When I added up the electoral votes in the 24 states likely to be in the **Romney camp (plus one from Maine)**, I got **204 total electoral votes**. When I added up the electoral votes in the 19 states likely to be in the **Obama camp (plus three from Maine)**, I got **236 electoral votes**. As you can see, winning more states doesn't necessarily mean you get more electoral votes. If each state got one vote (remember our discussion of states' rights), Romney would probably be assured of a victory.

However, under the Electoral College system, it takes 270 electoral votes to be elected president. The eight still-undecided "swing states" held 95 electoral votes, enough to change the outcome.

As I followed the campaign, and the spring turned into summer, the polls continued to show the two candidates neck-and-neck nationally, but of course, the national vote mattered little - it was the voters in the swing states that would determine who the next president would be.

Analysis of the Swing States

After analyzing each state and determining how each was likely to vote, it seemed very likely that the deciding votes were going to come from the following eight swing states: Colorado (9 electoral votes), Florida (29 electoral votes), Iowa (6 electoral votes), Nevada (6 electoral votes), New Hampshire (4 electoral votes), Ohio (18 electoral votes), Virginia (13 electoral votes) and Wisconsin (10 electoral votes).

If Obama won the 19 states likely to be in the Obama camp, Romney would have to win most of the swing states in order to become the next president.

In **Florida**, the state that was the final battleground for Electoral College votes in 2000, the summer polls were showing the race to be very close. There were always enough undecided voters to change the outcome. Before 2008, Florida had always gone for the Republican presidential candidate (except in 1996 when the state went for a Southerner, Bill Clinton). In 2012, as in 2000, the Florida governor was a Republican, Rick Scott. Scott was a wealthy venture capitalist (like Romney). He ran for governor on a very conservative platform, spending 75 million dollars of his own money to get elected. He had the support of Jeb Bush, George Bush's brother who was Florida's governor during the controversial Florida 2000 presidential election. Scott had partnered with George W. Bush to buy the Texas Rangers baseball team so he was *in* with the Republican power brokers, and as a new governor, he would try hard to deliver the state for Romney.

Virginia was another state that, until 2008, had gone with the Republican presidential candidate. In this year's election, the question was, did Obama win that state in 2008 because the voters liked him, or was it a vote against the weak economy left by the Republican administration of George Bush?

Even if I assumed Florida and Virginia would go back to their tradition of voting Republican, that would only give Romney 246 electoral votes, not even close to the 270 required to win.

Wisconsin had recently elected a very conservative Republican governor, Scott Walker. But when he tried to ban public employee unions, a recall effort was put on the ballot to remove him from office. He managed to stay in office by defeating the recall, but the Democrats in Wisconsin were galvanized and ready to work hard for Obama. Wisconsin had a long history of voting for Democratic presidential candidates, and it looked like winning Wisconsin would be an uphill battle for Romney. It seemed likely Obama would add Wisconsin's ten electoral votes to his tally, giving him 246.

Nevada and **New Hampshire** had a history of sometimes voting for the Republican candidate and sometimes voting for the Democratic candidate. With the polls showing a near tie in both states, it was all but impossible to predict which way they would go in 2012. With similar electoral votes (six in Nevada and four in New Hampshire), there was a good chance they would cancel each other out if one went for the Republican candidate and the other for the Democrat.

Colorado and **Iowa** both had a history of voting for Republican presidential candidates. Assuming those two states continued to vote Republican and Romney added Colorado's nine electoral votes and Iowa's six electoral votes, he would still only have 261.

Add in **Ohio**, the state that (before 2008) only voted for a Democratic presidential candidate if he was a southern governor (Carter and Clinton), and it would give Romney 273 electoral votes, enough to win the presidency. It looked like the 2012 presidential election would come down to whether the states that had traditionally voted Republican would continue to do so. If so, Romney would be president.

But it's not that easy to unseat an incumbent president. The main reason the race was so close was because the economy had not improved as much as Obama had promised it would during his last campaign. In fact, when the University of Colorado did its usual analysis of the presidential race (based mainly on economic data from past presidential races), they found Romney to be the likely winner.

As the campaign moved through the summer, the polls continued to show a very close race. But Obama was consistently holding a slight lead in Ohio, a state with a large number of electoral votes. With Ohio, Obama would have a nearly insurmountable lead in electoral votes. If

Obama was to win Ohio, Romney's path to victory would become much more difficult.

The problem for Romney in Ohio was that many people who lived there were very dependent on jobs related to the auto industry (one in eight jobs in Ohio were connected to the auto industry), and Romney was on the record saying the automakers should have gone through bankruptcy proceedings before being allowed to get government help. His reasoning was that they needed to rid themselves of burdensome debt before restructuring. Obama had decided in favor of a direct government investment in the automakers. General Motors and Chrysler got direct government investment. They didn't have to go through the Chapter Eleven bankruptcy process, and that helped keep the unemployment rate in Ohio relatively low. (Ford did not get government aid, and neither did the foreign-based auto companies like Toyota and Honda that manufactured vehicles in the U.S.)

The Campaign: Significant Events

One way to look at the 2012 presidential campaign is to look at the events that the candidates hoped would "move the needle" in terms of changing voter attitudes. Below, I summarize the main issues and events that evolved during the 2012 presidential campaign.

The Economic Argument

In the summer of 2012, the polls were showing a near dead heat in the presidential race. However, when the polls asked which candidate would better solve the nation's economic problems, Romney consistently came out ahead - but only if the respondents were male. When the same question was asked of female voters, Obama always came out ahead.

There were also differences in the polling data depending on which demographic group was polled. Among polled voters who identified themselves as Hispanic, Obama consistently lead by a margin of nearly two to one. Among polled voters who identified themselves as African-American, only three percent said they would even consider voting for Romney.

In every speech, Romney talked about the stubbornly high unemployment rate, pointing out that far from delivering an improved economy, as President Obama had promised in 2008, the unemployment figures had grown worse since he had taken office four years before. In response, Obama pointed out the fact that it was Republican policies under George Bush that had put the economy into such bad shape in the first place. He said the economic situation would be much worse without the policies he had put in place.

Romney laid out a five point economic plan which he said had been endorsed by many of the nation's top economists, including five Nobel laureates. He said his plan's five main goals were 1) making the U.S. energy independent; 2) getting more people into job training programs; 3) opening more free trade with Latin America; 4) cutting the deficit; and 5) reducing taxes on the middle class. In response, Obama said the numbers in Romney's plan just didn't add up.

Neither candidate's argument seemed to sway many voters. The polls continued to show a near dead heat, and in every poll, there were always enough undecided voters to change the outcome either way. One thing was evident, the current state of the American economy was going to be a significant issue in both candidate's campaign.

The 47% Video

On May 17, Romney met with supporters for a dinner at the Boca Raton, Florida home of Marc Leder, a financier. Although Romney was not yet the party's nominee, he agreed to have an informal discussion with the guests about his chances against president Obama, as long as the participants in the discussion agreed not to release his comments to the media.

However, unbeknownst to him, someone in the room was secretly making a video of his comments. The homeowner later said he suspected the video was made by one of the catering staff, and said he was considering legal action as the video was released to the media without his permission and without the permission of the many people who appear in it.

The video maker *did* turn out to be a member of the catering staff. Understandably, he wanted to remain anonymous, but he was known to several members of the media who reported that he was anti-Romney.

The video was kept secret for some time, but on September 17th, Mother Jones magazine published an article titled "SECRET VIDEO: Romney Tells Millionaire Donors What He REALLY Thinks of Obama Voters: When he doesn't know a camera's rolling, the GOP candidate shows his disdain for half of America."

The article included a clip from the video in which Romney is heard to say " . . . there are 47 percent who are with him [Obama], who are dependent on government, who believe they are victims, who believe the government has a responsibility to care for them . . . ."

The national news media picked up the story and for several weeks it was mentioned and the video was shown nearly every time Romney's name came up.

At first, Romney said his comments at that dinner were speculative and that they hadn't come out exactly the way he wanted them too. But later, he completely disavowed what he had said at the dinner, saying in no way did it reflect his true feelings. That did little to stop members of the media from using the video against him, and the Obama campaign from frequently mentioning it.

The secret video turned out to be the first issue in the campaign to have an effect on voter opinion. Nationwide, and in the key battleground states, the polls showed voters turning against Romney. Commentators on TV began to talk about an inevitable Obama victory.

Anti-American Demonstrations and the
9-11 Attack in Benghazi, Libya

Early in September, 2012, someone in the U.S. put together a short, very amateurish video that poked fun at the founders of the Muslim religion and posted it on the YouTube internet site. Although few people had actually seen the short video clip, it set off a series of anti-American demonstrations all over the world. From Egypt to Australia and in some European countries, there were protests and burnings of the U.S. flag. In countries like Yemen and Tunesia, the protests turned violent.

After several U.S. embassies were attacked on September 11th, the anniversary of the 9-11 attacks in New York in 2001, government officials in Washington, and elsewhere, were closely watching the situation. However, when reports starting coming in that the U.S. diplomatic mission in Benghazi, Libya was under attack, there was apparent confusion about what was going on there. The attack ended with four Americans dead, including U.S. Ambassador J. Christopher Stevens.

Although al-Qaeda claimed responsibility for the attack, in the weeks that followed, representatives of the Obama administration were saying it was just another protest against the anti-Muslim video that had gotten out of control. In the middle of a closely contested presidential election, such an event was bound to come under close scrutiny, which brought Obama's entire foreign policy with regard to the whole Middle East into question.

When video was released, showing that there were no demonstrations in that area of Benghazi and that the men who attacked the embassy were heavily armed, some people began to suspect that the Obama administration was trying play down the attack. They suggested the attack showed that anti-American extremists were well entrenched in Libya, despite the administration's support of the uprising there that had removed Libya's leader. The president strongly denied that accusation, but the attacks from Republicans continued. They included accusations that Stevens and others had been worried about just such an attack, because of other recent attacks in the area, and that they had asked for more security. But his requests had been denied. In fact, instead of providing more security to the embassy, some of the existing security forces had been pulled out, apparently to show trust in the new Libyan government.

Eventually, the facts came out. There was no demonstration. The attack was a well-coordinated mission, pre-planned to take place on 9-11. Reports surfaced that the attackers were militants related to al-Qaeda, and that the group included seasoned al-Qaeda fighters that had been brought in from Tunisia and Iraq.

There is still some confusion about exactly what happened, but it is now known that at about 9:40 in the evening on September 11th, a large number of bearded men, wearing the type of Afghan-style tunics favored by Islamic militants, sealed off the streets leading to the U.S. Consulate in Benghazi by setting up roadblocks composed of pickup trucks mounted with heavy machine guns. According to eyewitnesses, the trucks bore the logo of Ansar al-Shariah, a group of Islamist militants who had worked with the municipal government to provide security. The attackers arrived in front of the compound, that served as the U.S. embassy, carrying an extremist flag and shouting, "Allah Akbar." They stormed the compound from multiple directions. They used heavy weapons to penetrate the outer perimeter of the compound and drove back the few U.S. and Libyan security forces that were stationed there. The Libyan guards just inside the gate were beaten but not seriously injured.

An unarmed U.S. Predator drone was immediately moved into position over the compound to monitor the situation in real time, and emails were sent to Tripoli and to Washington D.C. saying the compound was under attack.

As soon as they heard the attack begin, the ambassador and one of his security agents took refuge in a barred "safe haven" room. The attackers didn't find them there, but before they left, they set the building on fire. The security agent escaped, but the ambassador did not. It was later learned, he died from smoke inhalation.

A quick reaction force, at first described as State Department contractors but later confirmed to be CIA contractors, were at a nearby annex. About 25 minutes after receiving the first call for help, they put together a convoy to go to the compound to save the ambassador. They were unable to find him in the smoke-filled building, so they left. On the way back to the annex, they came under attack from militants using machine guns and hand grenades. Somehow, they made it back to the annex despite two flat tires. At that time, the annex also came under attack from gunfire and mortars.

At about one o'clock in the morning, almost four hours after the attack, local citizens (some reports called them looters) found Ambassador Stevens's body, apparently still alive. He was rushed to a local hospital in a private car, but doctors there pronounced him dead.

The next day, the Libyan government denounced the attack, and there were protests against whoever had carried out the attack.

President Obama announced that they were trying to track down the killers. He also announced that he was beefing up security at all U.S. facilities in the region.

But that didn't end the controversy about the attack. Critics said the Obama administration had tried to cover up the true nature of the attack because it might reflect badly on U.S. foreign policy in the region. Republican lawmakers started hearings on the matter.

President Obama, and other members of his administration, denied that there had been any sort of cover-up. They said they had not been given correct information about the true nature of the Benghazi attack from intelligence sources.

Nevertheless, the Benghazi attack and the aftermath continued to be a topic of dispute throughout the rest of the campaign.

The First Presidential Debate

The first presidential debate took place on October 3rd. The subject of the debate was supposed to be domestic policy and the moderator was PBS commentator, Jim Lehrer.

The president went first, saying he had created five million jobs in the private sector, that the auto industry had come roaring back, and housing had begun to rise. He said the nation needed to invest more in education and attacked Romney for his unwillingness to raise taxes on the wealthy. He said America does best when the middle class does best.

Romney was eager to talk about the economy. He mentioned the rapid rise in the deficit, and he described people who had come up to him with stories of lost jobs and difficult times. He again laid out his five point plan and hammered home the concept that the president had failed to fulfill his 2008 campaign promises. He reminded the voters that Obama had promised to cut the unemployment rate in half, while in fact, unemployment had gotten worse. He said when the president took office, 32 million people were on food stamps and now there were 47 million people on food stamps. He said economic growth was slower this year than last year, and last year was slower than the year before. He added, "Going forward with the status quo is not going to cut it for the American people who are struggling today."

President Obama did not respond directly to those issues, but instead said we need to make an investment in new forms of clean energy. Also, he said he wanted to provide tax breaks for companies investing here in the United States instead of abroad. He pointed out that it was the previous Republican administration that had created the economic problems and that Romney wanted to take us back to reduced taxes on the rich and fewer regulations on Wall Street. He said that he had been working to reduce the deficit, pointing out that under his administration 77 government programs had been cut, including military aircraft programs. He said he had cut eighteen government programs for education that were well-intentioned but weren't helping kids learn. He said he had aggressively gone after medical fraud in Medicare and Medicaid and had saved tens of billions of dollars. He again attacked the numbers in Romney's five point plan.

Romney disputed Obama's characterization of his five point plan and said his goal was both to lower taxes on the middle class and to create new jobs. He said he would close tax loopholes and work toward energy independence through the use of clean coal and by increasing offshore and Alaskan oil drilling.

Obama again attacked Romney's economic plan and added that the governor had changed some aspects of it. He said that for eighteen months Romney had been running on his new tax plan, and now, five weeks before the election, he was saying that his big, bold idea was "never mind." He added that under Romney's plan, people like Donald Trump would be defined as a small business.

On the topic of entitlements, Romney attacked the president's reduction of payments to providers. He added that Obama was going to take huge amounts of money out of Medicare to pay for his new "Obamacare" program. (He apologized for using the term "Obamacare," but the president said he had come to actually like the term.)

Finally, Romney said he would get rid of unnecessary government subsidies such as the subsidy to public television. He said he liked

PBS, in fact, he loved Big Bird, but he didn't want to keep on borrowing money from China to pay for it.

After the debate, polls of registered voters who had watched the debate on TV said Romney had "won" the debate (although many didn't like him saying he would stop subsidizing Big Bird). Even Obama supporters said the president seemed lackluster and low key, while Romney seemed fired up and more aggressive.

But a poll of TV viewers is not the same as a poll of voters. The real question was whether Romney had cut into Obama's lead as a result of the debate. Within days, the answer was loud and clear - he had. After the first debate, Romney closed on Obama in the polls nationwide and in the crucial swing states.

In the days after the first debate, Romney continued to gain in the polls. Political commentators began to backtrack on their comments that Obama was sure to win. In fact, some polls indicated Romney had pulled ahead in Colorado, Florida, New Hampshire, and Virginia, but not by very much. A few polls suggested Romney had even pulled ahead in Ohio, but most polls showed Obama holding onto a narrow lead there.

In the follow up to the debate, Obama often referred to Romney's comments about cutting off support to Big Bird, and the Democrats released a campaign ad criticizing that statement.

The Romney campaign said the Democrat's focus on Big Bird was an act of desperation and an unwillingness to talk about how Obama's four years in office had failed to help the struggling economy.

Many in the media disputed parts of what both candidates had said in the debate, but Romney continued to gain in the polls. Most commentators were surprised that one debate could change people's minds about the two candidates that much. Some suggested that Romney's surge in the polls was simply a response to the fact that he had stood toe-to-toe with the president and had held his own. Luckily for Obama, there were still two debates to go.

The Vice Presidential Debate

The only vice presidential debate took place on October 11th between Vice President Joe Biden and the Republican vice presidential nominee, Representative Paul Ryan. Martha Raddatz of ABC News was the moderator.

Many Obama supporters hoped Vice President Joe Biden would be very aggressive to make up for the president's lackluster performance in the first presidential debate. And he was. Not only did he attack Republican policies at every opportunity, but he laughed out loud and made faces while Ryan talked, calling Ryan's comments "a bunch of malarkey" and "a bunch of stuff."

Much of the debate was about economic policy. The term "middle class" was used more than twenty times during the debate

Although there was some discussion about whether Iran had been allowed under Obama's watch to get closer to having a nuclear weapon, there was little new ground covered in the debate.

After the debate, the media made more of Vice President Biden's behavior than anything either of them had said. Obama's supporters applauded Biden's aggressive approach, while many Republican's said he had acted like "a buffoon." They said they liked Ryan's more reserved, more professional, demeanor.

One issue the post-debate media did focus on was the vice president's response to the moderator's question about the Obama administration's handling of the tragic attack on the U.S. diplomatic compound in Benghazi. The moderator had asked why it took so long for the administration to admit it was not a spontaneous demonstration over an anti-Muslim YouTube video, but rather a planned attack by extremists on the anniversary of the 9-11 attacks on the twin towers in New York City. The vice president responded that they were just going on what the intelligence agencies were telling them.

After the debate, many Republicans were saying that after the terrorist attack in Benghazi, Libya, both the president and the vice president had tried to cover up a failed policy in the Middle East by saying it was only a spontaneous demonstration that had turned violent. The Obama critics asserted that the attack was obviously a planned mission with advanced weapons and tactics. They said it clearly showed al-Qaeda was as strong as ever in the area which meant Obama's feat of having him killed didn't amount to anything.

Despite the accusations, in the days following the vice presidential debate, neither the national polls nor the swing state polls showed much change. Obama still held a slight lead nationally, but Romney was closing.

The Second Presidential Debate

As the date of the second presidential debate approached (October 16th), most commentators were still focused on the president's poor showing in the first debate. Would he snap back and be more aggressive? Many of his supporters were insisting he would. They said he would hit Romney hard on his comments that had been captured in the secret 47% video. They insisted Romney's surge in the polls had not been due to the policies he had laid out, but due to a poor "performance" on the part of the president. They said the moderator, Jim Lehrer, had not done enough to rein in Governor Romney (even though an analysis of the debate showed Obama had held the floor longer).

The second debate was to be "town-hall" style. That is, both candidates would be on their feet answering questions from an assembled audience of potential voters. The moderator would be CNN political commentator, Candy Crowley, and some Obama supporters predicted she would try to rein in the aggressive debating style Romney had used against the president in the first debate. She had selected questions from those submitted by the assembled audience (but the audience members who were selected got to read their own questions).

In this second debate, President Obama turned out to be the more aggressive debater. As his supporters had hoped, he came out swinging. He even did what his supporters had been urging him to do; he referred to the secret 47% video, saying Romney had, behind closed doors, said that ". . . 47 percent of the country considers themselves victims who refuse personal responsibility - think about who he was talking about: folks on Social Security who've worked all their lives, veterans who've sacrificed for this country, students who are out there trying to, hopefully, advance their own dreams, but also this country's dreams, soldiers who are overseas fighting for us right now, people who are working hard every day, paying payroll tax, gas taxes, but don't make enough income."

The first question from the audience was from a college student who was worried about finding a job after he graduated. Obama answered his question by saying he would build more manufacturing jobs in this country, and immediately attacked Romney for recommending the government "let Detroit go bankrupt." He added that he would change the tax code to give incentives to companies to invest here in the United States.

When it was Romney's turn to answer the young man's question, he referred to Obama's economic record and pointed out the fact that 23 million people were still struggling to find a job. As in the first debate, he again brought up the high unemployment rate in the country. Then he defended himself against the president's charge that he let the auto industry go bankrupt, saying it was the president that had actually taken General Motors and Chrysler into bankruptcy.

At that point, the moderator interrupted Romney to let Obama respond.

Obama responded that if they had done it Romney's way, it would have meant the loss of a million jobs.

Romney countered that if the auto industry had been allowed to go through bankruptcy like 7-Eleven, Macy's, and Continental Airlines, they would have come out stronger.

Obama said that what Governor Romney said just wasn't true. He repeated that Romney's approach would have lost a million jobs. He then went on to again attack Governor Romney's five-point plan, saying he didn't really have a five-point plan; he only had a one-point plan which was to make sure that folks at the top play by a different set of rules. He said under Romney's plan you could make a lot of money and pay lower tax rates than somebody who makes a lot less, you could ship jobs overseas and get tax breaks for it, you could invest in a company, bankrupt it, lay off the workers, strip away their pensions, and still make money.

Romney tried to respond, but the moderator cut him off.

Another question from the audience was about the rising gasoline prices. Obama said he had raised oil production and supported alternative sources of energy. He then returned to attacking Romney, saying Romney's plan was "to let the oil companies write the energy policies."

Romney disputed Obama's figures about increased oil production and said that although he also supported the development of alternative sources of energy, he would do more drilling, and issue more permits and licenses, and allow more use of clean coal.

Obama's response was that "very little of what Governor Romney just said is true." He went on to say the best energy strategy was an "all of the above" strategy.

The two candidates then went into an extended, toe-to-toe, back and forth session of one-liners interrupting the other and disputing what the other had said. The moderator tried to intervene but was unable to.

Finally, she tried to get Obama to stop so the next question could be asked to him.

But Romney said it was his turn, and then he went on to dispute the last thing the president had said.

When the moderator finally was able to regain control, she said the next question was for Governor Romney, and it was about taxes.

Romney answered by presenting a long list of statistics that he said proved President Obama's policies were failing. In summary, he said his plan would result in lower taxes for the middle class.

Obama disputed Romney's figures, saying, as president, he was the one who had made life better for the middle class. He then attacked Romney for saying on a recent 60 Minutes TV show that he wanted to cut taxes on the very rich.

Romney responded that he wanted to cut taxes for everybody, and that cutting taxes on the rich would help create jobs.

Obama said Romney's plan was vague. He spoke directly to Romney and said, "you were a very successful investor. If somebody came to you with such a sketchy plan that was going to cost seven or eight trillion, you wouldn't have taken it, and neither should the American people because the math doesn't add up."

Romney responded by saying his figures did add up, and he went through the figures again. He said it was the president's math that didn't add up. He said the president's plan would put us on the road to Greece (at the time, the Greek economy was in very bad shape).

The next question was from a woman who asked about what the candidates would do to help women get equal pay to men in the workplace.

Obama answered by telling about how his grandmother had worked in a bank but had hit the "glass ceiling." He said one of the first things he had done as president was to sign the Lilly Ledbetter bill, a bill that allowed women to bring suit against companies that denied women equal pay.

Romney responded by saying when he had been the governor of Massachusetts, he had asked women's groups to help him find qualified women to serve in his cabinet. He said the women's groups had brought him whole binders full of women, and he had ended up with more women in the state's senior leadership positions than any other state in America. He also said, that in his administration, he had allowed women to work flexible hours so they could go home and make dinner for their kids when they got home from school.

Obama responded that Governor Romney feels comfortable having politicians in Washington decide the health care choices that women are making.

Another questioner referred to the lack of economic progress over the past four years.

Romney repeated his five point plan, saying it was designed to get small businesses to grow and hire people.

Obama responded more directly to the question, saying he had inherited a tough economic situation when he took office. He referred to George W. Bush's failed economic policies and added that Governor Romney's policies would be even worse.

The next question was similar to the previous one; the questioner said he had voted for Obama in 2008 but felt less optimistic after Obama's four years in office.

The president responded by laying out his successes, passing the health care bill and creating 5 million jobs. He reminded the questioner that he had gone after al-Qaeda's leadership like never before, and that Osama bin Laden was dead. He added that Romney would not be willing to raise taxes on the very rich.

Romney responded by reminding the questioner that the last four years hadn't been as good as the president had just described, and that the next four years wouldn't be much better. He said that in 2008, Obama had promised to lower the unemployment rate to 5.4 percent, but had failed to do that. He said Obama had promised to put forward a plan to reform Medicare and Social Security, but he hadn't even made a proposal on either one. He said Obama had promised that middle-income families would have a reduction in their health insurance premiums, but instead they had gone up. He said the middle class had been crushed during Obama's four year tenure (which was a near quote of a statement that Vice President Biden had said in a speech, that the middle class had been "buried the last four years").

There was a question about illegal immigration, and Romney responded by saying he would put in place an employment verification system to make sure employers didn't hire people who had come into the U.S. illegally. He said he would not give driver's licenses to those that have come here illegally, as the president would.

Obama responded by saying "We are a nation of immigrants." He said he had streamlined the legal immigration system to make it easier for people to come into the country legally. On the other hand, he said he had put more Border Patrol on than anytime in history, and the flow of undocumented workers across the border was lower than it had been in the last 40 years

That discussion was followed by a tense exchange over whether Romney had a history of exporting jobs overseas.

Both candidates more or less ducked the question of whether they would put new gun control laws into place.

Then came a question about why the State Department had refused extra security for our embassy in Benghazi, Libya.

The president responded that he knew the families of the foreign diplomats personally, and that nobody was more concerned about their security than he was. He said the perpetrators would be tracked down. He said "one of the things that I've said throughout my presidency is when folks mess with Americans, we go after them." Then he criticized Romney's response to the attacks, saying he had just tried "to make political points."

The question about the Benghazi attacks was undoubtedly the question Romney had been waiting for. He said he felt very deeply sympathetic for the families of those who had lost loved ones, but then he went on to criticize Obama for going to Las Vegas for a political fundraiser the day after the attack and for not being forthright about the fact that it had been a planned attack and not simply a protest about an anti-Muslim video that had turned violent. He said members of the Obama administration had continued to characterize the attack that way, instead of admitting it was a planned attack on the anniversary of the 9-11 attacks on the twin towers in New York, and that it had been carried out by well-trained and well-armed extremists. He said it called into question the president's whole policy in the Middle East.

Obama rejected the idea of a cover-up, saying the day after the attack, he had made a speech at the White House in which he told the American people that this "was an act of terror."

Romney seemed surprised at the president's statement and questioned it.

Obama refused to comment further.

Romney pressed the issue, saying he wanted to get Obama's statement on the record because the truth was he hadn't said it was an act of terror; in fact, it had taken the administration fourteen days to admit that. Romney insisted the president had never called it an act of terror.

Obama interrupted, saying, "Get the transcript," and Ms. Crowley added, "He did in fact, sir."

Obama quickly said, "Can you say that a little louder, Candy?"

The audience broke their vow of silence and applauded the president's statement.

It was a difficult moment for Romney. It seemed to throw him off track. He wanted to dispute Obama's statement, but the moderator had supported Obama, and that left Romney struggling to find a way to continue the discussion about the Benghazi attack as an indication of Obama's failed policies in the Middle East. He referred to statements by other members of Obama's administration that said it was not an attack, but merely a demonstration about a video that had grown violent. But if what the moderator had said was true, that Obama had indeed called it an act of terror, then Romney's suggestion that there had been a cover-up would not work.

The moderator did try to undo her overt support of Obama's statement by quickly agreeing with one part of Romney's statement, saying, "He did call it an act of terror. It did as well take two weeks or so for the whole idea of there being a riot out there about this tape to come out. You are correct about that."

After the debate, there were mixed opinions about which candidate had won, but most agreed that the president had been far more aggressive, and to many, that meant he had won. Much to the delight of his supporters, he had even taken the opportunity to attack Romney with regard to the secret 47% video as part of his closing statement by saying, ". . . he said behind closed doors that 47 percent of the country considers themselves victims who refuse personal responsibility - think about who he was talking about: folks on Social Security who've worked all their lives, veterans who've sacrificed for this country, students who are out there trying to, hopefully, advance their own dreams, but also this country's dreams, soldiers who are overseas fighting for us right now, people who are working hard every day, paying payroll tax, gas taxes, but don't make enough income."

Because it was part of Obama's closing statement, Romney did not have a chance to respond.

After the debate, there was considerable discussion in the media about two things, Romney's "binders full of women" statement, and the moderator's seeming to take Obama's side during the debate.

With regard to Romney's "binders full of women" comment, some Massachusetts women's groups were quick to say that they had provided the binders full of qualified women's resumes without being asked.

With regard to the moderator's taking sides, some media outlets were quick to provide transcripts of the statements the president had made the day after the Benghazi attack. They pulled out the specific section that included references to the Benghazi attack and insisted he had been speaking about terrorism *in general*, and was referring more to the 9-11 attacks in New York in 2001 than the Benghazi attack. Here is a transcript of that section of his talk:

" . . . yesterday was already a painful day for our nation as we marked the solemn memory of the 9/11 attacks . . . As

Americans, let us never, ever forget that our freedom is only sustained because there are people who are willing to fight for it, to stand up for it, and in some cases, lay down their lives for it. Our country is only as strong as the character of our people and the service of those both civilian and military who represent us around the globe. No acts of terror will ever shake the resolve of this great nation, alter that character, or eclipse the light of the values that we stand for."

Only the president knows whether he was referring to the Benghazi 9-11 attack, or the New York City 9-11 attacks of 2001, when he referred to "No acts of terror," but Ms. Crowley did make a half-hearted apology after the debate, saying the president had not actually made reference to the Benghazi attack as an act of terror as she had maintained during the debate. She blamed her mistake on the words Romney had used, and anyhow she was only saying the president had indeed used those words.

After the second debate, everyone was waiting for the next round of polls to see if the president had stopped the momentum Romney had gained after the first debate. As before, the polls were mixed, but still very close. Even if the president had stopped Romney's momentum with his aggressive debate tactics, it was clear that it was still a very close race.

The third debate was to be held only a few days later, and both candidates spent most of their time preparing for it, with a few campaign stops in the swings states in between.

The Third and Final Debate

The third and final debate was on Oct. 22nd in Boca Raton, Florida, and it was to be on foreign policy. The moderator was Bob Schieffer from ABC News.

The subject of the debate was supposed to be foreign policy and the moderator's first question was about what had happened in Benghazi, Libya.

Romney began by broadening the discussion to turmoil in the Middle East in general. He said Arab Spring uprisings had brought a great deal of hope, but instead we've seen, in one nation after another, a number of disturbing events. He mentioned 30,000 civilians killed in Syria, the terrorist attack in Libya, and the fact that the northern part of Mali had been taken over by al-Qaeda types of individuals. He added that Egypt now had a Muslim Brotherhood president. He also brought up Iran, saying they were now four years closer to having a nuclear weapon. He congratulated the president on taking out Osama bin Laden, but added, "We can't kill our way out of this mess."

Obama responded by saying his first job as commander-in-chief was to keep the American people safe. He said he had ended the war in Iraq and refocused attention on "those who actually killed us on 9/11." He said al-Qaeda's core leadership had been decimated. He said, with respect to Libya, as soon as he had received "that phone call," he immediately made sure that everything was done to secure the Americans who were still in harm's way. He said that he would investigate exactly what happened and go after those who killed Americans. He added that he had taken leadership in organizing an international coalition so Libya could be freed of dictatorship "without putting troops on the ground."

Romney said it was good to go after the bad guys, but his approach was broader than that. He said Arab scholars had said the Middle East needed more economic development, better education, gender equality, the rule of law. Romney said that meant the U.S. should provide foreign aid and direct foreign investment. He said that had not been happening. He said there was a rising tide of chaos with al-Qaeda and other jihadist groups rushing in.

Obama didn't respond to that. Instead, he attacked Romney, accusing him of saying Russia was the threat, not al-Qaeda.

Romney disputed Obama's accusation, saying Russia was a geopolitical foe.

Obama interrupted him, saying "Number one."

Romney went on to say Iran was the greatest threat and Russia and Mr. Putin had stymied U.S. efforts in the UN time and time again.

He then tried to bring up the subject of whether some U.S. forces should have been left in Iraq, but the president interrupted him again, saying, "That's not true."

That led to an extended argument about who had said what about how many U.S. troops should have been left in Iraq.

The moderator tried to bring order back, but was unsuccessful. Obama continued to accuse Romney of making untrue statements in some of this campaign speeches and how he was now trying to back away from them.

Romney didn't agree with the president's accusations, but didn't seem willing to attack back. In fact, he often agreed with the president. He agreed that going after Osama bin Laden had been the right thing to do. He agreed that restraint was the best policy with regard to Syria, and he agreed that we should set a deadline to get out of Afghanistan. He also agreed that the president had been right to say it was time for President Mubarak of Egypt to go, and he agreed that we should maintain our shaky relationship with Pakistan. He did say the U.S. should have taken more of a leadership role in Syria, but the president disagreed and said he *had* taken a leadership role there.

President Obama said Governor Romney had proposed wrong and reckless policies. He said Romney had praised George W. Bush as a good economic steward and Dick Cheney as somebody who had shown great wisdom and judgment. He said Romney would take us back to the kinds of strategies that got us into this mess.

To that attack, Romney only chuckled. He said he had a policy for the future. And then he changed the subject to the U.S. economy. He said he knew what it would take to create 12 million new jobs and rising take-home pay. He said what we've seen over the last four years is something he didn't want to see over the next four years. He then reiterated his five point economic plan.

Obama responded by attacking Romney's leadership as governor of Massachusetts, saying that when Romney was governor, small businesses development in the state ranked 48th out of the 50 states. He also attacked Romney's policies on education while he was the governor of Massachusetts.

When Romney tried to respond, the moderator said they should get back to foreign policy, but he did relent and gave Romney time to respond to the president's attack about Massachusetts education. Romney simply quoted statistics which he said ranked the Massachusetts' education system as among the best in the nation.

Obama interrupted him, saying, "That happened before you came into office."

Romney started to defend his education policies as governor, but the moderator said he had already heard this in prior debates and wanted to shift the conversation back to the topic of defense spending.

Romney added that he would balance the budget, but Obama said Romney's numbers "just didn't add up."

Romney said they should get back to the topic of defense spending, but Obama wanted to continue to talk about the numbers in Romney's economic plan.

When the president was finished attacking Romney's numbers, Romney merely said he *would* balance the budget, but they should get back to the subject of defense spending. He said the U.S. Navy was smaller now than any time since 1917. He said the Air Force was older and smaller than any time since it was founded in 1947.

Obama responded by saying Governor Romney hadn't spent enough time looking at how our military works. He said, "You mentioned . . . that we have fewer ships than we did in 1916. Well, Governor, we also have fewer horses and bayonets."

At this, the audience broke their vow of silence and laughed. Then the president reminded the audience that he was the commander-in-chief by adding, " . . . when I sit down with the secretary of the Navy and the Joint Chiefs of Staff, we determine how are we going to be best able to meet all of our defense needs. . . . and that is not reflected in the kind of budget that you're putting forward, because it just don't work." The moderator tried to interrupt, but Obama added, "And you know, we've visited the website [referring to Romney's website] quite a bit. And it still doesn't work."

The moderator was then able to get the two candidates back on track with a question about Israel and Iran.

Obama went first, saying, "Israel is a true friend. It is our greatest ally in the region." He said he had put together a coalition that had imposed sanctions on Iran and it was working. Then he again attacked Romney, saying the governor would take premature military action, and it would be a mistake to put young men and women in harms way.

Romney responded that when he became president he would stand with Israel. He said that five years before he had laid out seven steps at the Herzliya Conference in Israel, and then he outlined a few of those steps, saying they included sanctions against Iran. He said military action would be his last resort. He went on to say the president had started his presidency with an apology tour of the world. He said that projected weakness to our enemies.

Obama replied, "Nothing Governor Romney just said is true." He emphasized that he would make sure Iran didn't get a nuclear weapon.

Romney again said Iran was now four years closer to developing a nuclear weapon.

After the moderator asked what was the greatest future threat to the national security of this country, Obama said it was terrorist networks, but then he immediately changed to the subject of China, pointing out all he had done to rein in China. He seemed to be responding to Romney's statement in the previous debate that China was a currency manipulator.

Romney replied that companies had shut down and people had lost their jobs because China had not played by the same rules.

Obama used that statement to attack Romney. He repeated what he had said in the second debate, that Romney, as a businessman, had been shipping jobs overseas to China.

Romney replied that ". . . attacking me is not talking about an agenda." He also responded to Obama's prior assertion that he had wanted to shut down the auto industry. He said he was "a son of Detroit." He said he had been born in Detroit when his dad had been the head of a car company. He said, "I like American cars. And I would do nothing to hurt the U.S. auto industry." He reiterated that it would have been better to take the auto companies through a managed bankruptcy so they could get government help and government guarantees.

Obama interrupted, saying , "Governor Romney, that's not what you said."

When Romney tried to defend himself, Obama again interrupted, saying, "Governor, you did not."

Romney said, "That's the height of silliness," and Obama replied, "Let's check the record."

They argued back and forth until President Obama said, "Governor Romney, you keep on trying to . . . airbrush history."

Romney replied, "You're wrong. You're wrong, Mr. President."

Obama replied, "No, I am not wrong."

Romney replied, "You're wrong."

Obama replied, "I am not wrong."

Finally, the subject was changed back to the economy. Romney said he didn't want to go back to the policies of the last four years. He quoted statistics, such as the fact that incomes had declined every year for middle-income families during the president's term in office, down $4,300. He said 23 million Americans were still struggling to find a good job. He said, "When you came into office, 32 million people on food stamps - today 47 million people on food stamps." Romney went on to say that when Obama came to office, the country was just over 10 trillion in debt, and now it was 16 trillion in debt. "You said by now we'd be at 5.4 percent unemployment. We're 9 million jobs short of that." He added that it was not going to happen by just hiring more teachers. He said, "I love teachers." He said he didn't think it was up to the federal government to do the hiring of teachers. He repeated, "I love teachers. But I want to get our private sector growing, and I know how to do it."

At that point, the moderator said, "I think we all love teachers." That got a big laugh from the audience. He then asked the two candidates for their closing statements.

The president went first. He said, "You've now heard three debates, months of campaigning and way too many TV commercials."

That got another laugh from the audience.

He went on to say that he had made real progress digging out of policies that gave us two prolonged wars, record deficits, and the worst economic crisis since the Great Depression. He said Governor Romney wanted to "take us back to those policies: a foreign policy that's wrong and reckless; economic policies that won't create jobs, won't reduce our deficit, but will make sure that folks at the very top don't have to play by the same rules that you do." He went on to say that as commander-in-chief, he would maintain the strongest military in the world, but that after a decade of war, it was time to do some nation building here at home.

When it was Romney's turn, he said he was optimistic about the future. He said that there were two very different paths the country could take, one represented by the president that would raise the national debt and head the country toward the situation Greece was in. He said he would get the country on the track to a balanced budget, while the president's path would mean continuing decline in take-home pay with 20 million people out of work. He said he would get people back to work with 12 million new jobs and get people off of food stamps by getting them good jobs.

When this last debate was over, the discussion began again about which candidate won. As with the previous debate, there was agreement that Obama had been the aggressor by far and that meant, for many, that he had won the debate.

There was a lot of talk about Obama's frequent insults of Romney, especially about his saying Romney was "wrong and reckless." There was also a lot of discussion about Obama's comment about "horses and bayonets" in response to Romney's saying we needed a bigger navy. Some reminded the president that the Marines do still use bayonets. Others thought that kind of comment would help Obama nationally but might hurt him in the important swing state of Virginia because of the many shipbuilding jobs there.

Some news agencies went to the trouble of counting up how many times the president had interrupted Governor Romney, but most still thought Obama had won the debate (maybe *because of* how often he interrupted and/or attacked Romney).

Some observers pointed out the many errors or misstatements that had been made during the debate, but most of the post-debate talk was about how passive Romney had been. He didn't use the Benghazi attacks as much as most thought he would, and he seemed to agree with most of Obama's foreign policy decisions. Sometimes he didn't bother to respond to Obama's insults, saying only that "Attacking me is not an agenda." Some people speculated that Romney felt that since he had momentum in the polls, all he had to do was act presidential.

The poll results after the debate indicated the race was still very close, but there were some indications that Obama's aggressive tactics in the last two debates had at least slowed Romney's momentum.

Countdown to the Election

After the third debate, on the campaign trail, President Obama kept up his relentless attacks on Governor Romney. In his campaign speeches, he tried to portray Romney as an out-of-touch rich man who wanted to take the country back to the Republican policies that had caused the current economic problems. He said Romney was only interested in helping the rich, and that he would destroy Social Security and Medicare.

In Romney's campaign speeches, he kept the focus on the president's record. He said Obama's 2008 campaign slogan had been "change," but now he wanted to "go forward" with no change. Over and over again, he recited statistics that he said showed the country had gone backward economically instead of forward during Obama's four years in office.

He often referred to Obama's pledges to help the economy during his 2008 presidential campaign. Romney said the president had kept none of those promises. He also spoke a lot about Obamacare, which he said would steal money from Medicare and would reduce payments to doctors which, he said, would make doctors refuse to take on new patients. In his post-debate campaign speeches, Romney tried to sound more moderate, often referring to his good record as a moderate governor of Massachusetts.

Obama started using the term "Romnesia" to suggest Romney's new attempts to sound more moderate meant that he had forgotten some of the more conservative stances he had taken during the Republican primaries in order to get the conservative Republican vote.

COMMENT:

Some of the very conservative Republican senatorial candidates were not helping Romney's attempts to sound more moderate.

> Republican tea party favorites were taking a hard line on abortion and illegal immigration, and the Democrats were using Romney's endorsement of those candidates against him.

After the debates, the campaign trail was almost entirely a back and forth path between New Hampshire, Iowa, Ohio, Virginia, and Florida, with frequents trips out west to Colorado and Nevada. The other 43 states were pretty much ignored (except when the candidates needed to raise money). In the past, presidential candidates tended to focus more on getting the majority of the people in the U.S. to vote for them, but in an election this close, both candidates put their time and energy into getting the only votes that would really count, the Electoral College votes from the swing states.

The president's main strategy in the last few weeks of the campaign was to attack Romney. He often attacked Romney's record as governor of Massachusetts saying Romney had imposed new taxes on everything from gas and milk to marriage and birth certificates (here, Obama added the line, "which would have been expensive for me," a joking reference to the so-called "birther conspiracy" that had forced him to release his Hawaiian birth records). Obama constantly tried to link Romney to the failed economic policies of the Bush administration. At a rally in Virginia, he said, "We can't afford to go backwards to the same policies that got us into this mess; we've got to go forward with the policies that are getting us out of this mess." He continued to mock Romney's job-creating plan as "nonsensical and insubstantial." In Richmond, Virginia, he said, "I've got a plan that will actually create jobs, not just talk about creating jobs, a plan that will actually create middle-class security, not just use the words." He added, "Unlike my opponent, I'm actually proud to talk about what's in my plan, because the arithmetic works." He also came out with a new, glossy pamphlet that described his existing jobs proposals, which, he said, had been blocked by the Republican-led House of Representatives.

Campaigning at the same time in Virginia, the Republican vice presidential nominee, Paul Ryan, ridiculed Obama's pamphlet as meaningless and described it as a "comic book." Some Republicans described it as a slick re-packaging of "more of the same."

Meanwhile, Romney mocked the president's 2008 campaigning slogan of "Change" by saying the president was now championing "no change." He said the president was proposing "more of the same" policies that had the country stuck in a weak economy. He said what the country needed was "big change."

Obama replied that Romney may be calling for "big changes," but all he was really offering was a return to policies that failed in the past. He said they were actually "a repeat, a relapse," of things that didn't work in the past and wouldn't work now.

COMMENT:

Throughout the campaign, the candidates and/or their wives were often seen on TV. In addition to appearances on all of the national TV news networks, Obama appeared on most of the TV talk shows, including The View, the Tonight Show, Late Night, the Letterman show, the Jimmy Kimmel Show, the Steve Harvey Show, the Daily Show, the Oprah Winfrey Show, the Daily Show, and others

Meanwhile, Governor Romney was noticeably absent on TV, appearing on very few scheduled TV shows. Ann Romney and one of her sons did appear on "The View," a weekly TV show hosted by a panel of women. The women questioned Mrs. Romney on abortion and access to contraception, and one of the women on the panel, Whoopi Goldberg, pointed out that none of the Romney men, including Mitt Romney and his sons, had ever served in the military. She suggested the reason Mitt Romney had never been inducted into the armed forces during the Vietnam era was because his Mormon religion got him a religious deferment. She said the Mormon religion didn't allow men to go and fight. Ann Romney replied that many, many members of the Mormon faith had served in armed services. Later, Goldberg came under a lot of criticism for her remarks, but she dismissed them as "racist name calling."

Meanwhile, in his campaign speeches, Romney constantly tried to bring the discussion back to the president's record. He often quoted statistics that he said showed how bad Obama's economic plan had been. Sometimes he did try to defend himself against Obama's attacks, saying Obama's campaign "seems to be smaller and smaller by the day. Attacking me is not an agenda for the future." But mostly, he spoke about the president's record.

In a speech in Iowa, he said, "Four years ago, candidate Obama spoke to the scale of the times. Today, he shrinks from it, trying instead to distract our attention from the biggest issues to the smallest, from characters on Sesame Street and silly word games to misdirected personal attacks he knows are false."

Surprisingly, with the country's longest war still going on, there was little campaigning that had anything to do with foreign policy issues (except for the recent attacks on the U.S. consulate in Benghazi.

The Green Party presidential candidate, Jill Stein, was getting some national attention by talking about war and foreign policy. She pointed out that President Obama had dramatically increased the frequency of deadly attacks by U.S. unmanned drones and that he had spread the drone attacks to Yemen and Somalia. She said the drone attacks had resulted in 75 percent of Pakistani civilians believing the U.S was their chief enemy, not the Taliban or al-Qaeda. She said the drones were killing far more innocent civilians than true terrorists and that fact was being used as a very successful recruiting tool by the terrorists. She said it was the drone attacks and other foreign policy decisions that Obama had made during his four years in office that were responsible for the recent anti-American protests all over the world.

Meanwhile, Fox News was trying to keep the Benghazi attacks of September 11th in the news. They pointed out that a reporter had gone to Benghazi on September 15th, four days after the attack, and had found Ambassador Stevens's personal journal in the wreckage of the U.S. consulate buildings in which he reported that he had been worried about just such an attack and had been asking for more security. The fact that a reporter could find such a thing, days after the attack, showed the consulate site still had not been secured. Fox News questioned whether there really was any investigation going.

At the same time, Congressional investigations were underway in which Republican congressmen were strongly condemning the administration's handling of the situation. Several Republican members of Congress sent letters to the Obama administration demanding more information about the Benghazi attack.

The Obama administration said the issue was under investigation and accused Romney of politicizing the situation in Libya. In fact, in the latter days of the campaign, Romney said little about Benghazi, the Middle East, or foreign policy. Instead, he preferred to keep the focus on what he called the failed Obama economic policies.

COMMENT:

The changing demographics of the United States was to play an important role in the 2012 presidential election. In the last two U.S. censuses, the number of people that identified themselves as of Hispanic origin had increased dramatically. In fact, Hispanics accounted for more than half of the nation's growth in the last decade. That was sure to hurt Romney's chances because the 2012 polls were showing that only 20 percent of Hispanics polled said they were planning to vote for him.

The 2010 census also showed that the segment of the population that identified themselves as black or African-American had increased from twelve percent of the population in 2000 to over sixteen percent in 2012, and nearly all of the polled African-American voters said they were planning to vote for President Obama.

In addition, because of the design of the Electoral College, even non-voters were to play a role in the 2012 presidential election. Since 1964, the number of electors has been fixed at 538. **States are assigned electors based on their total population, not the number of eligible voters**. The number of electors assigned to a state are recalculated before every presidential election based on the most recent census. States gain electors if their populations increase, which means electors have to be taken away from states whose populations have not increased. In 2012, it is notable that states like

---

Arizona and Texas gained electors. **Since the presidential election of 2000, Arizona has gained three electors, and Texas has gained six electors.** Those nine electors were taken away from other states that did not have such large increases in their populations. It is known that much of the increase in population in Arizona and Texas is due to the influx of undocumented people from south of the border. Therefore, in 2012, we had the unusual situation that some states gained electors even though they did not gain voters.

The Polls

As the election campaign entered its last few weeks, the polls were showing the race couldn't be closer in the all important swing states. In Nevada, all of the polls had Obama in the lead, but by only a few percentage points.

In Colorado, Romney had a slight lead in some of the polls, and Obama had a slight lead in other polls.

In Iowa, the polls were showing Obama with a slight lead.

In the crucial state of Ohio, Obama had been holding a small lead in the polls throughout the campaign. But in the final two weeks, there was a dramatic difference in the polls. Some showed Obama with a big lead, while others showed the two candidates in a tie.

In New Hampshire, Romney had a slight lead in some of the polls, and Obama had a slight lead in others.

In normally-Republican Virginia, the polls were mixed, with some showing Romney with a slight lead, while others showed Obama with a slight lead.

In Florida, most of the polls were showing Romney with a very slight lead.

The media was full of Electoral College analysis. With the Electoral College lead Obama was likely to build up in the states with the largest number of electors, it looked like Romney would have to win Florida, Virginia, and Ohio, plus at least two of the other traditionally-Republican swing states to become president.

After both campaigns were suspended for several days due to the huge hurricane that hit the upper East Coast, the candidates engaged in nearly non-stop campaigning in the swing states.

COMMENT:

In some past presidential elections, there have been last minute events that may have changed the outcome. Known as an "**October surprise**," events such as Henry Kissinger's statement just days before the 1972 election that "peace is at hand" in Vietnam helped assure Nixon's reelection despite the news that was starting to come out about the Watergate break-ins. Another example came about in 2000. Just days before the election, it was reported that Republican presidential candidate George W. Bush had once been arrested for drunk driving (Gore won the popular vote, but Bush became president anyhow by winning the Electoral College vote).

An October **non-surprise** took place in the presidential election of 1980. The Iran hostage crisis had dragged on for years and was hurting incumbent Jimmy Carter's chances of being reelected. Carter thought he had a last minute deal to free the hostages before the election, but the deal fell through. Later, the president of Iran revealed that Reagan's campaign aides had struck a deal with Iran to delay the release of the hostages until after the election. Reagan denied it, but the later arms-for-hostages scheme in Iran carried out by members of Reagan's executive branch gave credence to the idea.

As the 2012 presidential campaign neared its end, there was widespread discussion as to the likelihood of an October surprise in such a close and hard-fought election.

As it turned out, the only October surprise was the weather. An unusual fall hurricane hit the upper East Coast the week before the election. President Obama canceled his scheduled appearances in hard-hit Virginia, and his campaign aides said it would only be fair for Romney to also cancel his scheduled appearances. Romney announced that out of respect for those who were suffering from the hurricane's impact, he would cancel all of his campaign appearances until the crisis was over. He went to Ohio to organize a relief effort to send food and clothes to the hardest hit areas.

As a result, the president got to be constantly in the news by holding many official press conferences about the government's ongoing disaster relief effort while little was heard from Romney.

For a few days at least, the media stopped reporting on the election and focused only on the hurricane's aftermath. It did seem to give the president a slight boost in many of the polls, but whether it had any affect on the outcome of the election is still an open question.

Chapter Seventeen
Conclusions

Although the country has grown dramatically both in size and in population, **presidential elections still operate under rules created when the United States was made up of only thirteen small states**, many of which were almost entirely rural.

At first, the outcome of presidential elections were likely to be influenced by things like a candidate's record in wartime, or his personal history, in addition to his stance on policy issues such as slavery or westward expansion.

Eventually, **electronic media coverage began to be more important** in presidential elections. How the candidate handled himself on radio or TV became about as important as his stance on policy issues.

Today, with nearly **instantaneous media coverage of just about every utterance a presidential candidate makes**, elections have become media-driven events. The candidate that gets the most "air time" is usually the winner. But **access to the media costs money**. As a result, the candidate that wins the popular vote is often the one who can raise the most money.

The 2000 presidential election showed that in a modern election that is closely contested, the presidential candidate that wins the most votes in the general election may not get to be president. In 2000, **George Bush** became president even though **Al Gore** won the general election by 543,895 votes.

For much of the 2012 presidential campaign, there was ongoing discussion about whether what happened in 2000 would happen again this time. Throughout the campaign, the candidates (and therefore, the media) focused on a handful of states that they believed held the key to winning the Electoral College vote. Never before in U.S. history had there been so much attention on the workings of the Electoral College.

This time everyone was aware that the popular vote was irrelevant. When, late in the campaign, the nationwide polls began to get closer and closer, some even started to suggest that the Republican, Mitt Romney, might win the popular vote, but lose to Obama in the Electoral College. That seemed unlikely to me because the polls were still showing Obama with a big lead in states like California and New York, states that seemed sure to deliver him huge margins in the popular vote. On the other hand, the states where the polls were showing Romney in the lead had much smaller populations (except for Texas).

The Outcome of the 2012 Presidential Election

As I looked at the polls in the final days of the 2012 presidential campaign, it seemed to me that Obama would win the popular vote, perhaps by a large margin, and squeak out an Electoral College win. That is, if he could win the key swing states of Colorado, Iowa, Virginia, Florida, and most importantly, Ohio.

In the end, that is exactly what happened. Obama won the popular vote by about two million votes (thanks to the east and west coast states) and squeaked out enough wins in swing states to retain his presidency.

President Obama lost two of the states he had won in 2008 (Indiana and North Carolina), but he held onto the other swing states. However, his margins of victory in those swing states was much lower than in 2008: in most of them, he won by less than two percentage points, and as in the 2000 presidential election, Florida was a near tie.

The final polls before the election showed the race to be a dead heat in the swing states. So what happened? There was a lot of post-election discussion about what had moved the voters toward Obama. Most of the talk focused on three subjects that seemed to be a liability for Romney: his religion, the 47% video, and the "October surprise" hurricane that seemed to stop Romney's momentum. Overlooked in this analysis was the change in the country's demographics. Among voters that identified themselves as Hispanic or African-American (the fastest growing segment of the population), Obama won overwhelmingly. Also, as compared to past elections, far more women voted Democratic in 2012 (this may have been due more to the Republican party's platform than to Romney's likeability.)

Most people will remember the 2012 presidential campaign as the first in which there was far more focus on the potential Electoral College outcome than on the outcome of the general election. They will remember it as the year Mitt Romney *almost* became president even though Barack Obama won by winning a handful of key swing states.

They will also remember it as the most expensive presidential campaign in history. As the campaign neared its end, the news media reported that more than six billion dollars had been spent by the two candidates, most of it in only nine key swing states.

It seems to me, the 2012 election is going set the pattern for most future presidential elections. Now, both the Republican and Democratic parties have access to almost unlimited amounts of money. As a result, presidential elections are bound to be closer and more contested from now on.

So, what have we learned from the presidential election of 2012? It seems to me that the main thing we learned was that until we get rid of the Electoral College, presidential elections are going to be decided by a small number of voters in a few of the so-called "swing states." The rest of us are going to be relegated to the role of onlooker.

INDEX

About The Author

Dr. Everett Murdock is an Emeritus Professor at California State University, Long Beach.

www.ingramcontent.com/pod-product-compliance
Lightning Source LLC
Chambersburg PA
CBHW070952040426
42443CB00007B/468